*Turn South
at the Second Bridge*

Turn South
at the Second Bridge

LEON HALE

TEXAS A&M UNIVERSITY PRESS

College Station

Library of Congress Cataloging in Publication Data
Hale, Leon.

    Turn south at the second bridge.

    Reprint of the ed. published by Doubleday, Garden
City, N.Y.
      1. Texas—Social life and customs—Anecdotes,
facetiae, satire, etc. 2. Country life—Texas—
Anecdotes, facetiae, satire, etc. 3. Texas—Description
and travel—1951- —Anecdotes, facetiae, satire, etc.
4. Hale, Leon. I. Title.
[F386.6.H3 1980] 976.4 80-5517
ISBN 0-89096-100-X

Manufactured in the United States of America

With gratitude to all those who
sat and talked . . .
And with love to Helen, who did all
the hard part.
L.H.

"I doubt he'll be home this time of day, but if you want to drive out there just stay on Fifty-nine till you pass the first country church about six miles out. Then take the blacktop east and watch for a white house with a screened porch across the front. Generally you'll see a few old glass-eyed cow dogs layin' around there under a big live oak just inside the fence. About a quarter mile on east, then, you'll want to take a red dirt road runnin' south off the blacktop. That'll swing you around through the woods to where you're headed nearly west. Count your creeks and turn back south when you cross the second bridge. You'll drive right to it then, because the road leaves off there. I'd say don't get out of the car till you raise somebody in the house, on account of the dogs. If you happen to miss it, ask anybody. Main thing, remember to turn south at the second bridge."

—From the directions of a thousand feed-store and filling-station men.

Turn South
at the Second Bridge

PREFACE

I am writing this sentence with a pencil on May 17, 1980. A few weeks from now when I see it set in type, probably I won't much like it. I'll growl at the thing, I expect, and wonder why I didn't make it sound better. I am talking to you now out of thirty-four years' experience in the writing game. Since 1946 I have been making modest sums of money for composing sentences. In that time I have produced mighty few that I was entirely satisfied with by the time they were printed and circulated where I couldn't get them back and patch them up.

The reason I mention this here, I want to get credit for standing firm against the awful temptation that confronts me now. This book is about to be reprinted, and it contains thousands of sentences I wrote in 1963, seventeen years ago. I have the itchy feeling that most of them ought to be rewritten before they are sent out into the world again. But the publisher cautions me that this is a reprint, not a revised edition, and I mustn't start rewriting. So everything stands as it came out of me in '63.

A few minutes ago I finished reading the book for the first time in I think fifteen years. On every page I found sentences that beg to be recomposed. Some of them give me active pain.

That may sound as if this little volume is not dear to me. It's dear to me, all right. It was my first book and I love it the way a parent loves a first-born child. It may represent, when I finish up, my most significant and worthwhile work. But if I were doing it again, I would make some changes. Mostly I would leave out some things I put in.

In '63 I still had a tendency to try to fool readers into thinking that I was comfortable using four-bit words. *Sobriquet*, for example. And *soporific*. I am astonished to run across those creatures in a book I wrote. I'm not even on speaking terms with them, and I don't like their looks. But they must stay in. Try to skip over them.

Even worse, somewhere in chapter 1 you will meet up with the dreadful phrase *washed down*, used in the sense that a meal was washed down with drink. I consider that to be the least tolerable of all the clichés I see in Texas newspapers and hear on television. "Guests at the barbecue consumed fifteen hundred pounds of brisket . . . washed down with copious amounts of beer." That gags me.

Beginning shortly after I wrote this book, for ten years I posed as a teacher of writing. I met with students and graded their stories. I gave an automatic *D* to anyone who wrote that food was washed down with drink. What an embarrassment to find that nauseous expression in my own stuff. Evidently it had not begun nauseating me in '63.

At that time I seemed also hung on the terms "humming railpoint" and "bustling community." I was unable to have a railpoint that didn't hum or a community that didn't bustle. And I was describing parts of rural Texas with such stuffiness as "wolves still abound" there.

Something else I blinked about, in chapter 12 I let Shorty Hale saw off on me the story about the blind mule, and I set it down just as if it hadn't ever happened before in the world. By '63 I expect that tale was already a standard item in the folklore of at least forty states.

Mild inaccuracies occur in these stories. They don't amount to much and I won't correct them. It doesn't seem to matter that it was the Lyric Theater, not the Majestic, where I watched horse operas back in my old hometown. In chapter 1 I indicated that the bar in Scheller's Place at Glen Flora came out of a saloon. I've since learned it was a soda fountain bar in a drugstore. So be it.

In the late 1950's and early 1960's I was fearless about making strong, unqualified statements in print. Such as the one in chapter 8: "Port Aransas is the best town on the Texas shore to bum around in during winter." Remember that fifteen or twenty years ago I was a great deal smarter than I am now. I knew things then that I can scarcely dream of in 1980. I even knew things that weren't so. I am not saying the statement about Port Aransas is false. It might have been true in 1963. I do not believe it is now.

Because a lot can change in seventeen years. Early in the book you'll find the statement that Texas voters spoke loud and clear and said they didn't want liquor sold by the drink in their state. Since then they spoke again and said they did, at least on a local option basis. So Texas is now pretty well equipped in the matter of saloons, especially in the larger cities.

If I were revising I would probably change my comments about rural blacks. Somewhere I referred to "Texas plantation Negroes" as "gentle, fun-loving people." I don't feel that's an inaccuracy, because in my view those I referred to were, in fact, gentle and fun-loving. But that sort of statement sounds patronizing to me now and I don't care for it. In the seventeen years I have become more sensitive about racial matters.

I could list dozens of changes that have come since '63, to date these stories. You mustn't, for instance, go to Madi-

[3]

sonville and expect to find the honeybees still swarming out of the courthouse walls. That building is gone, destroyed by fire, and replaced by a courthouse I don't like as well as I did the old one.

You'll also find references to fifty-cent country haircuts and men getting ready to go to the moon and rural real-estate prices as high as $250 an acre. I'm not sure what that fifty-cent haircut costs now. Three or four bucks, I expect. You already know that those men finally got ready to go to the moon and went, in 1969. Probably you know too that a huge crowd of buyers would be attracted by any good piece of rural real estate priced as low as $250 in 1980.

Readers who have found pleasure in this book press me sometimes to name my own favorite part of it. Usually I pick one of the storytellers and say his tale is the one I like best. Most times I say it's Welcome Woods's story of how the Model A ran away with him and his cousin that night between Hearne and Milano. Other times I'll say it's Pat Craddock's story about cooking whiskey in the Navasota Bottom, or the sermon Virge Whitfield preached to me over the hood of my car, just outside his garden gate.

Several of the minor incidents described have, over the years, become special to me. The most astonishing quotation from a Texan that I ever copied down is in this book, in chapter 9. It's Johnny M.'s statement about his career as a professional thief.

In chapter 12 is a brief and inadequate description of the pain on the face of a twenty-six-year-old pulpwood worker, while he tried to puzzle out the meaning of three simple words in large type. The pain was there because he couldn't read, and wanted to so much, and I can remember seeing nothing so poignant as that.

Also in chapter 12 you will find Will Weeren standing

on the boardwalk in the little town of Burton and reciting for me the poem "Invictus." In the book I gave that five lines. It has become a significant scene to me because of the finality it represented. I mean, shortly afterward Will Weeren was gone. So was the boardwalk. So were the store buildings it fronted. And I knew that never again would anybody stand on a boardwalk in a Texas country town and recite a William Ernest Henley poem.

That's true also of the others, so many of them. Nobody else will ever ride in a buggy, asleep and alone, while her sorrel horse takes her to town the way Miss Annie Spinn's mare took her into Brenham from her country home. Nobody else will ever take cars across the river by the power in his shoulders, the way Fred Jenkins was doing at Sheffield Ferry on the Angelina the last time I saw him.

That's what makes me glad now about the contents of this little book. When I was trying to make a record of these events and people and places and scenes, I didn't realize that so many of them were final things.

Leon Hale
May, 1980

FOREWORD

In Leroy and Toodle Levien's little café in Carmine, on the twentieth day of January in 1959, I was having fried chicken on the lunch when Leroy himself mentioned to me that he would be closing up for a couple of hours at one-thirty.

By way of explanation he handed me without comment a small sheet of paper about five by seven inches, all bordered in black. It was an announcement saying that funeral services would be held at 2 P.M. for Mrs. Annie H. Afflerbach—"aged 81 years, eight months, and four days."

Such funeral announcements are yet common items around the small towns of Texas. Towns like Carmine, population 950. You see them posted in conspicuous places—on the front windows of general merchandise stores, on the counters by café cash registers, even on the doors of recreation parlors—to explain why these establishments are temporarily closed.

In the country towns of Texas people in the main have not forgotten to love their neighbors, and most merchants still close up shop during funerals as a way of honoring departed friends. This custom was once followed everywhere in my state, but then the cities got so big it wasn't practical and of course you can't expect cities to honor departed friends unless it's practical.

Anyway, by one forty-five, there in Carmine in 1959, every business in town was locked up and most of the 950 citizens were gathering in quiet bunches outside the little white Lutheran Church.

I don't know yet why I decided to go in. I am a guy that generally runs from funerals. I had never met Mrs. Annie Afflerbach or any of her relatives. It was just that I was in Carmine, and everybody in Carmine was going to the funeral, so when the service started I slipped in and took a back seat. Every pew was filled.

"'Let not your heart be troubled . . .'"

The pastor began with that familiar passage out of the 14th Chapter of St. John so often read at funerals, and I remembered that long ago, when I was a youngster and was taken to the last rites of kinfolks, I heard that passage many times and wondered what it meant.

"'In my Father's house are many mansions: if it were not so I would have told you.'"

Well, it was a simple service of great beauty, with songs from the small choir, and all the right and proper and comforting words from the pastor.

There is something about a sermon preached at a funeral that gets next to you as regular Sunday sermons seldom do. I doubt that the pastor preaches any better. I think it's because people listen better. When they come to a funeral they don't do a lot of jawing and visiting and looking around to see what everybody is wearing, and they never go to sleep as some do in regular church.

So they sit and look straight and listen, and hear the pastor touch upon a solid truth concerning every man—that one day all of us will pass on, just the same as the person whose funeral we are attending, and we don't know whether it will happen twenty years from now, or in six months, or in ten minutes—a thought that's apt to sober a person and set him thinking on matters he doesn't ordinarily think on.

After the service I sat out in my car in the mellow January sunshine for a long while. And I suppose because of the frame of mind this occasion thrust on me, I got to thinking of deep things, like The Past and The Future. In another fifty years, would the people of Carmine close up shop and all attend the funeral of a citizen who had lived in their community for eighty-one years, eight months, and four days?

No, I guessed they wouldn't. Because customs, like people, fade and die and are buried. Even in the short decade that I'd been traveling about to towns like Carmine, I'd seen the people and their towns and their homes and their farms and their stores and their schools changing, always changing. And the changes have continued at an even faster pace during the five years since that day I sat in the sun at Carmine.

And it suddenly struck me as a sad thing to know that one of these days nobody would really remember the people and the country towns in my part of Texas. At least not the way I'd want them remembered. Nobody would remember that Ed Scheller had an alligator that slept indoors by the stove, or that Jim Riley owned a white bull named Buster that suffered a nervous breakdown. Nobody would know how Ross Foley played the fiddle left-handed while customers honked for service out on the driveway of his filling station. Or how Paul Blankenship, the tugboat captain, talked when he sat in Aggie South's Grill telling about the greatest thing that ever happened to him. Or how Virge Whitfield would walk ten miles to pick up a stray dog and carry it home again to love it and feed it, or how Pat Craddock lost his left leg when the law caught him cooking whiskey. Nobody would really know how it was.

So I think it was then, in January of 1959, that I first thought of writing at least a part of it down.

Right now I'm not certain how many people are interested in knowing that J. B. Choate, in his country store near Alvin, once showed a nice profit by selling buffalo chips wrapped in cellophane for ten cents a package. It's just that someday somebody might want to know about it, and it wouldn't be recorded anywhere, and that would be a shame.

The places in this book are real. And the people are real, though it's possible and even likely that a few, since I last saw them, have had those proper words said over them in some little white church while the shops around town were closed.

Let me say, too, that these people are not typical (that awful word) of the country folks of Texas. Small-town and rural Texans can be every bit as conformist as the suburbanites of Houston and Dallas, and most of them are. My people, the ones in this book, you don't find on every post-office corner or behind every wire gap. They have the strength to be individuals and the courage to speak out and show that they are, in front of a guy they know is going to write down what they say. For this I admire them, and hold them in highest regard. I also thank them. They are the people that keep the color and the flavor and the character in Texas, at a time in its history that economics threatens to make it a chamber-of-commerce type state, advertising in national magazines to draw the money of tourists.

Most of these individuals I found, for indeed I had to search for them with the aid of a legion of helpful citizens, in the course of my work as a columnist for the Houston *Post*. This journal affords me the happy freedom to roam at will about the countryside, in search of whatever there is to find. For this I get paid. I add that because people sometimes ask.

My territory is referred to by economists and headline

writers as the Gulf Southwest, a great curving slice of Texas coastal geography which includes Houston and a mighty industrial complex. Beyond and around and among the oil derricks, the refinery stacks, and the chemical plants, the skyscrapers, the shopping centers, and the housing developments lies another, older, and different-flavored world. The character of its towns and people was patterned long before Texas drill bits found oil trapped around the underground salt domes, and before the U. S. Army Corps of Engineers dredged fifty miles up Buffalo Bayou and made a great seaport out of Houston.

I stay outside the cities—in the Piney Woods of East Texas, the Post Oak Belt of South-Central Texas, the flat Texas Coastal Prairies and the wonderfully mysterious lower bottoms of the Brazos, the Colorado, the San Bernard, the Neches, the Sabine, and the Guadalupe rivers. And along three hundred seventy miles of Gulf shore.

This is not the same Texas you read about in the ranch novels. That's West Texas, which I understand from the cowboy stories and television dramas is yet peopled by long-legged cowhands that roll their own and ride paint horses through the sagebrush. You know a funny thing? I lived the first twenty-five of my forty-three years in West Texas and never saw any sagebrush? Or if I did we called it by another name.

The coast of Texas, where I migrated in 1946 for economic and other reasons (I can't ride a horse) is not the American West. It's not the Old South, either. It isn't even the Southwest in the sense that Oklahoma, New Mexico, and West Texas are Southwest. It's more nearly a transitional region between South and West.

Life and times in the East Texas Piney Woods, nearly twelve million acres of timbered hills north of Houston, evolved from the Deep South. East Texas was a cotton, corn, and mule country originally, though it's livestock and chicken country now. And timber country, which it always was.

The Post Oak Belt, north and west of Houston, is held together chiefly by deep sand and scraggly oak timber and barbed wire fences, a good many of which need mending. The exceptions that the chambers of commerce show you aren't yet sufficient to disguise the real nature of the region.

The flatness of the Texas Coastal Prairies is sometimes broken by dark woods and marshes and growths of huge old live oaks waving Spanish moss. But as a general thing, and in the eye of a person searching for natural beauty, this prairie is some of the ugliest and dullest real estate in all of Texas. It is also some of the most valuable. The Spanish grazed cattle on this prairie before a steer ever set foot west of Fort Worth. The Texas cattle industry was born on it. So was the modern American oil industry.

In the 1820s, the settlers came along behind Stephen Austin, that stiff-collared, soft-handed gent who history insists is the Father of Texas, and fanned up the river bottoms and farmed Alabama and Georgia style, with slave labor. They didn't build any adobe houses or cowboy bunkhouses. Those were all farther west, and came later.

There is a strong national background consciousness among perhaps half the people of the Post Oak Belt and the Coastal Prairies, for this region is heavily sprinkled and in spots saturated with citizens whose roots lie in Mexico, Czechoslovakia, Poland, and Germany. Dr. Hugo Weige, for example, the magnetic healer who used his thought-wave process to treat my sick tomcat from a distance of seventy-five miles, lives in Austin County at Industry. German immigrants owned land there in 1831, five years before Texas won independence from Mexico.

I include this brief background only because such a great many people, at the mention of Texas, never think of it as a state with moss-hung oaks, pine-covered hills, rice fields, and sandy beaches, nor that it has people named not only Morgan and Watkins but also Afflerbach and Bucek. My part of Texas has always struck me as being happily unrepresentative of the public notion of what the state is like. Yet I offer no theory that the background and the nature of the region are what produced the kind of individuals I have met in it. I don't know.

All I know is, this is where I found them.

CHAPTER 1

"When that pup grinned at me, I recognized my missing lower plate in his mouth."
—Jim (River Rat) Riley

One spring afternoon I stopped at Glen Flora and went in Scheller's Place to catch up on the news. The news was bad. Ed Scheller's alligator had passed away.

This saddened my reunion with the folks at Scheller's, who for my money are some of nature's nobility. The quality they have that keeps me going back from year to year to be among them is genuineness. That is, they are what they are, and nothing else.

Around Scheller's, it doesn't matter who you are. Your name doesn't amount to any more than the double blank in one of Ed's battered boxes of dominoes. What does matter is what you show yourself to be when you are sitting there at one of Ed's tables. What you were yesterday, or last month, or ten years ago—it just doesn't matter.

But then you have to know a few of the names. There is the proprietor Ed himself. And his good wife, who for some reason is called Dick, and her sister Pud Joines, who helps run the place, and Constable Billy Blair, the fearless officer of the law.

Then there is Jim Riley, who lives just down the road from Scheller's on the bank of the Colorado River. Jim writes poems and has a white bull named Buster that suffered a nervous breakdown. You ought to hear about that one.

[15]

Scheller's Place is a lot of things. A domino hall, a coffee shop, a refreshment parlor, a gathering place. It locates next door to the post office in the little town of Glen Flora, on the Lower Colorado in Wharton County.

When a stranger walks into Scheller's, he can't tell who is running the place and who is just patronizing it. Ed and his wife and Pud Joines generally sit at the tables like everybody else, and one of the customers is just as apt to be behind the counter serving refreshments as Ed himself. Ed has more important duties, such as participating in one of the domino games or seeing after a multitude of sidebar projects he carries on out back of the place. Like feeding his small menagerie of animals and birds.

Scheller's Place is narrow and long, as refreshment parlors are apt to be. Down one side is a heavy old bar with stools. The tables line up on the other. The bar survives from the days when saloonkeeping was a leading industry in Texas, before the voters spoke loud and clear and said they didn't want their whiskey served by the drink in public places.

I can't tell you what the walls of Scheller's are like. I've never seen them. They're covered with museum pieces, chiefly artifacts of the community's past. But not necessarily. Ed Scheller is a broad-minded curator. If anybody has an item of interest he wants the public to see, he takes it down and puts it on display at Scheller's. Ed's dead alligator may be on exhibit there by now. The hide of him lay curing in the barn the last I saw of it.

When a local woman underwent an appendectomy a few years back, she ordered her appendix pickled in alcohol and added to the museum pieces in Ed's place. None of the regular customers considered this to be in poor taste. After all, as one of the domino players pointed out to me, it's a

[16]

handsome appendix and was removed by the most skillful and expensive of surgeons.

Among the wall exhibits at Scheller's is a white mailbox sort of concern. This box contains many of the literary efforts of Jim Riley, who writes under the pen name of River Rat. He composes poems, song lyrics, and stories both true and false. These flow from River Rat's pen in glorious, wordy script. The stories deal with such events as Jim losing his lower plate and how a dream revealed where to find it. Jim regularly submits these features to *Reader's Digest* to get them officially rejected, after which they are placed in the little white box for public consumption. Jim's stuff never gets published, but he prides himself that it is rejected by a publication with a mighty impressive circulation.

It's not that Jim writes to make grocery money. Even if he were penniless, which he isn't, he could live well off the progeny of his white bull Buster and the fat blue catfish that sleep not thirty feet from his back door, down next to the Colorado's undercut banks. Jim doesn't want money. He just wants to be in *Reader's Digest.*

When things get slow at Scheller's after dark, sometimes Jim and I drive to his place and sit on the gallery. It's a wonderful place to talk on a starry night. You can almost spit in the river from your chair. With the tomcats moaning under the house and the Colorado slipping silently by, Jim rocks and tries out his stories on me.

He's a wonderfully grizzled, white-haired, red-skinned Irishman, Jim is. College educated, they say, but Jim doesn't talk about that. He doesn't want to seem proud, and likes to pretend he doesn't take a bath very often.

"Several things bordering on the supernatural have happened to me in my life," Jim said one night. Then he told about losing his dental plate.

"Normally," he said, speaking not at all like a river fish-

[17]

erman who doesn't bathe, "I go out to the washhouse to clean my false teeth after I eat.

"Well, I was performing this task the other day when I was called inside to perform some little chore, and I left my lower plate on the bench by the washhouse. When I got back, the plate was gone. Now we've got a little old spotted puppy around here, and there this pup stood, right by the bench where I left the plate, wagging his tail and licking his chops. Now that was a hundred-dollar plate and I can ill afford to lose any hundred-dollar plates. So I said well, I'll just find out if that dog ate my plate, and I stepped inside and took the rifle off the wall."

Now Jim Riley is a kind soul and doesn't ordinarily go about shooting pups and performing post-mortems on them. But he was pretty well worked up over the thought of that dog consuming his lower plate. He let fly a slug that creased the dog, and it took off across the pasture. "Well," said Jim, watching the pup disappear, "there goes my lower plate."

Several nights later Riley slept fitfully. The prospect of replacing the dentures disturbed his rest. He dreamed. In the dream he was going out to milk his cow when the pup ran from under the washhouse, tugged at Jim's pant leg, and tried to pull him toward the washhouse.

Ignoring this gesture, Riley proceeded to his milking chore. As he milked, the pup reappeared, tugged at his trousers once more, opened his mouth, and grinned at Jim.

"When that pup grinned at me," Riley said, "I recognized my missing lower plate in his mouth."

The puppy returned to his hiding place under the washhouse as Riley woke from his dream.

"The dream was so vivid I couldn't get it off my mind," Jim said. "So I got me some jacks, jacked up that washhouse, and crawled under to take a look."

There under the washhouse he found his missing dentures, unharmed.

"The puppy," Jim concluded, "returned home, and now enjoys good health."

That pup came out of his traumatic experience somewhat better than Riley's white bull Buster, the one that had the nervous breakdown.

I've never heard Riley call himself a rancher, but he keeps a little herd of mother cows on his place. In normal times Buster and his clutch of females graze quietly on the small acreage surrounding the Riley homestead.

"My cows generally are docile and complacent," Riley was telling me one day as we stood by the garden fence and looked out over his modest holding. "They always look to Buster for guidance and protection should an emergency arise. And if any other bull attempts to invade his domain, Buster is as fierce and valiant a gladiator as you'll find in the bovine field."

As you can see, when Riley talks for what he thinks may be publication, he trots out his college vocabulary.

"But my neighbor, Eddie Sohrt, bought a billy goat as a pet for his children. The goat was installed in a corral about two hundred feet from my fence line. For three days after the goat arrived, the cattle were uncommonly restless. They couldn't see the goat, but his scent kept them walking the fence and pawing and snorting and bellowing."

Riley was in his pasture chopping out wolf weeds the day the billy goat got out of his corral and paid a visit to Jim's cattle. Never having seen a goat before, Buster was confused and bewildered at the black and shaggy beast that now approached him. The cows and calves drew in close behind Buster as if seeking protection. Their tails began to rise, higher and higher, until all tails were perpendicular to the backs of their owners. Buster shivered nervously. The

[19]

goat ambled within a couple of feet of the white bull's horns and gave a small bleat.

That did it. Buster's knees buckled for an instant. Then he wheeled and took off bellowing for the river. Riley's little herd exploded in stampede.

"They were absolutely in blind terror," Jim said. "They ran into sheds, over feed troughs, into anything in their path. The younger cows and the calves sailed over my fences. The old ones just ran through 'em. My old milk cow Daisy ran full speed into this woven wire fence around the garden. It gave about twelve feet and threw Daisy back on her rump. She got up and ran at the fence again. She tore out a section of wire and dragged it about a hundred feet before she broke free and disappeared over the horizon. Me? I headed for the house."

It took Riley three days to round up his cattle. Buster himself spent two days down the river.

"Finally he came sneaking in, his nerves all shot, glancing now and then back over his hindquarters. He'd lost weight, all right, but worse than that he'd lost the respect of the cows. When he'd approach one, she'd toss her head and walk off."

Obviously, Riley concluded, Buster had suffered a severe nervous breakdown. The bull has never quite regained the prestige he once enjoyed there in Riley's pasture. No more than a buzzard's shadow will spook him even now.

The neighbor obligingly got rid of the billy goat so Riley could remain in the cattle business. But Jim himself said he personally had to change his pattern of living on account of the stampede. That is, he had to start taking frequent baths, since he wants to be certain that Buster never again catches a scent that might even vaguely resemble that of a billy goat.

Riley, as well as Ed Scheller and others of the regular

bunch around Scheller's Place, normally hangs close to home. But occasionally they venture up or down the Colorado on pleasant little safaris to see old friends or revisit the scene of adventures experienced long ago. I have tagged along on some of these trips. A time or two we set out for Blue Rhone Bend in search of the sand bar on which Ed Scheller claims he once stood face to face with Big Mike.

Big Mike was a panther, a monstrous big panther that once roamed the Colorado Bottom in Wharton County, carrying off livestock and terrorizing the people. That was thirty to forty years ago, when the deep rich soil of the river valley was covered with sugar cane. It was Jim Riley that named Big Mike, since the cat needed a name to get in one of Riley's magazine yarns. Jim wrote the story of Big Mike, putting in some frills that should have happened even if they didn't, and sent it off to *Reader's Digest*. This was Riley's greatest literary triumph. The magazine kept his story for three months before returning it with a rejection slip. That, Jim said, was a near thing.

Ed Scheller claims to be the only man that ever faced Big Mike. Ed is a muscular, round-faced citizen. He must be up past sixty now, though I've never thought to ask him. He's not a tall man but he's strong, with plenty of the old moxie. Ed had taken a bunch of youngsters coon hunting one night. For fear one of the youths might be accidentally shot, Ed didn't carry a gun with him. He was standing on the sand bar at Blue Rhone Bend, with the boys behind him, and suddenly there was the panther. It sat not six feet from Ed's face in the edge of the canebrake, as a big tomcat might sit on the hearth and stare into the fire. Ed said he did the only thing he could think of. He beat the panther about the head and ears with his lantern, and this so startled the beast that it turned and crashed off through the brake.

Ed clings steadfastly to this story, though Riley and a number of others often challenge it. "Now how is it possible," they ask Ed, "for a man to beat off a panther with nothing but a coal-oil lantern?"

"Well," says Ed, "it was a damn good lantern."

On the safaris upriver we have never quite found the scene of that victory. We always seem to get sidetracked. For example, we might stop off at Egypt, a community a couple miles north of Glen Flora, to see if George Northington wishes to go along. But he will have company. The company will be Pete Prihoda, an accordion player, and Lee Walla, who runs a cotton gin in Fayette County.

Walla is a bass-fiddle player. I guess that's what he is. But his fiddle is like you never saw. It is homemade, and consists of a hoe handle hooked to a washtub and strung with a window-sash cord. Walla is somehow able to make this bass fiddle work about as good as store-bought kinds, and he and Prihoda come to see Northington at Egypt and stand around and play music just for the fun of it, whether anybody is on hand to listen or not. Northington often joins in with his harmonica on such good country tunes as "Redwing" and "Buffalo Gal," and this makes such pleasant listening that even though you are on safari after panther stories you will stand around patting your foot until it is too late to push on.

The closest we ever got to Blue Rhone Bend was Dave Hall's Store at Elm Grove. It was raining that day and therefore too wet for Uncle Ike Shorter to work his mule in the cotton patch. So there Uncle Ike sat out front of the store, waiting for an audience. He loves an audience. Uncle Ike is an ancient Negro who preaches funerals over dead mules. He is also an authority on the panther, having heard the beast squall on many dark nights.

Isaac Shorter is Uncle Ike's square name. His hair appears

glued in white, tight curls to his skull, and even behind his dark glasses you see a touch of nobility in his features. He wears dark glasses because he lost an eye many years ago when a mule kicked him. We once took up a collection around Scheller's Place to buy him a glass eye. I don't know whether he ever got it. The last I heard of the matter, somebody was going to write off and see what one cost.

Uncle Ike is a cotton farmer and an entertainer. His work clothes are his costume. This attire consists of patched blue denims, a tattered green gabardine shirt, and old dress shoes with the tops split for comfort and air-conditioning.

Jim and Ed got Uncle Ike to perform some of his old routine there in Hall's Store. For half a century he has entertained people in Wharton County. It was once the custom, when anybody's mule died, to send for him to preach the mule's funeral.

It's a pity that Uncle Ike's humor can't be reproduced with the printed word. But it can't. It is the genuine, the pure humor of the Texas plantation Negro, dating from the day when these gentle, fun-loving people drew their entertainment from their own imaginations. It's pretty earthy comedy.

Uncle Ike doesn't preach many mule funerals today, since there are few mules left in the Colorado Valley. When they were so plentiful that at least one a week died within walking distance of Elm Grove, he would plod to the scene, slow and dignified, and perform the mock ceremony.

For purposes of preaching these mule funerals, he created out of his fertile mind a family of buzzards who attended the mule's last rites. The reason for their attendance was to dispose of the animal's remains. As I say, it is pretty earthy comedy. There is Old Man Ward, the father buzzard. His children are Bill Quill, Dewey, Suzanne, Mariah, and Josiah.

[23]

I doubt that a person could enjoy or even understand Uncle Ike's mule funeral unless he had studied buzzards. In the Cross Timbers country of Texas, west of Fort Worth, where I grew up, I have spent many an hour squatted in a clump of oak shinnery, watching these ugly birds at their work. Buzzard watching was on the list of approved summer amusements, ranking just below channel-cat fishing and viewing the Saturday-afternoon horse opera at the Majestic Theater. Buzzards have a remarkable number of human traits. More human, I always thought, than most of the jerky, chalk-faced characters that cavorted across the screen of the Majestic on Saturday afternoons.

"Bill Quill," explained Uncle Ike in the prelude to his mule service, "tested all cases."

That is, it was this buzzard's responsibility to approach the dead mule and claw it, to assure the other members of the buzzard family that the animal was deceased beyond a reasonable doubt. Uncle Ike's version of how Bill Quill, cautious and cowardly despite his reputation for courage, approaches the dead mule and makes the test is one of the funniest pieces of acting I ever saw.

Uncle Ike imitates a buzzard to perfection. He spreads his arms and turns and banks and glides and seems more vulture than human. When acting the part of the buzzard on the ground, he twists his aged frame in such a way that he appears actually converted into a buzzard.

The spice of the funeral service is the sad soliloquy of the papa buzzard, Old Man Ward. That venerable bird is grieved with self-pity because he is over the hill, unable to compete in the scavenging. If this weren't so funny it might even be touching.

"I ain't able, boys," moans Old Man Ward. "My jaws done got weak and I'm all drawed up."

This sort of entertainment, I'm certain, would leave a

city theater audience mighty cold. But to me it seems to retrieve something long lost—a time when people of the creeks and the river bottoms carved their entertainment from their own environment, from the flying, crawling, free creatures that shared it with them.

This required imagination, ingenuity, ability, and practice. I see Ike Shorter, as a boy in patched overalls, rehearsing in a grassy clearing on a creek bank, viewing his reflection in the water of the stream to see if he looked as graceful as a buzzard looks in flight, as awkward as a buzzard on the ground. And working at it until he had it pat and perfect.

Yet not once did it ever enter his mind that he would become a paid entertainer. And of course he didn't. He performed to hear the laughter and appreciation of an audience sitting under an oak tree draped with Spanish moss. This fed his ego and his yearning for accomplishment. It never fed his belly.

Uncle Ike believes buzzards to be special things. He thinks they carry the souls of deceased animals, such as mules.

He said he once won an argument with a preacher about this matter. He was able to quote a passage of scripture that proved it. The passage, Uncle Ike said, is in the book of "Romes" and goes like this:

"The human soul goes back to mother dust, but the dumb brute soul wander in the air."

To Uncle Ike this signifies, plain and simple, that the souls of dead animals go winging around forever inside buzzards. I can't find any such passage in "Romes" or any other book of the Bible, but I have no doubt that Uncle Ike believes it is there, with every ounce of strength in his great old heart. And that I respect.

About the panther, Big Mike. There are the usual stories

[25]

that this beast yet wanders at night in the Colorado Bottom near Blue Rhone Bend. He wanders in flesh or in spirit, as you choose. Some say they hear him squall when the wind is right.

Others say the Colorado flood of 1913 ran the beast out of the country. Ed Scheller says this couldn't be so because he faced the panther following World War I, after he returned from France, where he fought for democracy with the 36th Division.

Uncle Ike told us how the panther worked. The thing squalled, he said, like a man yelling. Its purpose was to get a man to answer, whereupon Big Mike would creep toward the sound, calling repeatedly, muffling his squall by sticking his head near the ground. In this way he was able to make a man think he was still far away. With this trickery (yes, you wonder who saw the beast perform it) the panther was credited with killing several people. Uncle Ike can imitate the panther's squall. He gets down on all fours to stick his jaw into a small hollow of the ground. He then gives out a plaintive cry, aimed upwind. It does, at that, sound far away.

When a person returns from a safari up the Colorado with Ed Scheller and Jim Riley, he is hungry. So he is invited into the back room of Scheller's Place, where Ed's wife and her sister Pud have "thrown a little something on the table." When a guest gets up from that table, he is not hungry again for a week.

More than once I have walked into Scheller's to get a hamburger and ended up eating at Mrs. Scheller's private table in the rear sanctum. The "little something" is likely to include steak cooked to fork-cutting tenderness in rich gravy. Black-eyed peas with big sweet onions and hot tomato relish. Enough mashed potatoes to fill a dishpan. Hot corn bread and Jersey butter. All this is washed down with home-churned buttermilk that has a soporific effect on the consumer, causing him to walk short-stepped and humped over, like a stove-up bronc rider, out back of Scheller's Place to stretch in the shade of a big oak and wonder what the poor folks are doing today. Mrs. Scheller and Pud serve a meal meant for a man who has spent the day following a mule in the cotton patch.

On quiet afternoons I have sat at one of Scheller's domino tables, waiting for somebody to come in and use Ed's phone booth. Ed went to an almighty lot of trouble to have that booth installed, especially considering the phone in it won't work and never will. Unaware that at least 50 per cent of everything in Scheller's is booby-trapped, strangers sometimes shut themselves in that booth and try valiantly and vainly to contact the operator, while all the regular patrons sit stone-faced and pretend not to notice.

Waiting for such entertainment to happen, Ed often sits and talks about his boyhood, about such events as the time he was bitten by a huge cottonmouth moccasin. "I was just a little old kid, and this cottonmouth grabbed a hold of my toe. So I went runnin' to Papa and showed him where my toe was bleedin', and he got out his straight razor and his strop and his powder horn and he split my little toe open and poured it full of black powder. Never did give me the least bit of trouble after that."

Or about the time he fired at the field lark with his father's old muzzle-loading shotgun. I never before heard of a muzzle-loading shotgun, but then you hear of a lot of things around Scheller's you never heard of before.

"We lived at Nada when I was a kid and I was always after Papa to let me shoot his old gun. And I pestered him about it so long that finally he told me to take it and shoot it. So I went out and found me an old field lark scratchin' around a corn stalk and I let loose at him. Well, I think

[27]

Papa had that thing loaded with slugs. It bloodied my nose and pretty near broke my shoulder. I missed the field lark but I covered him up with clods and dirt, and he wiggled out and sort of shook the dust off himself and flew up on a fence post and said, 'At ol' gun'll KEEL ya.'"

And if you've ever heard a field lark speak from the top of a fence post, you know that's exactly what he did say.

The time was that I questioned what Ed Scheller ever did, outside of fighting for democracy in France, to deserve the kind of daily fare Mrs. Scheller puts before him. But there's this much you ought to know about Ed—he is soft in the heart. Loves wild things. Feeds and cares for crippled rabbits, coons, squirrels, possums, anything that's helpless. A man and a boy, walking along the Colorado, find a bird in the bushes with a broken wing. "What'll we do with it, Pa?" asks the boy. "Why," says Pa, surprised at such a question, "we'll take it to Ed Scheller and he'll nurse it."

Ed once raised a mama redbird that had free run of Scheller's Place. For three years it flitted about the establishment, causing all Ed's customers to keep their coffee cups covered with their hats. The bird even took baths in Mrs. Scheller's aquarium. Then one day something startled the poor thing and it flew into the electric fan.

That was sad. Not so sad, though, as the death of Ed's alligator. Ed raised the alligator from a baby. He just called the thing Alligator. By day Alligator soaked himself in a long metal water tray under the oaks out back. Nights he slept in a section of wooden pipe his benefactor built for him.

In winter, on chilly evenings when other citizens of Glen Flora go out and wrap their hydrants against the possibility of a freeze, Ed would go out and wrap Alligator up. Tuck him all snug and tight into his wooden pipe.

Texas coastal summers, hot and humid, were ideal for

Alligator and he grew at the rate of about twelve inches a year. The last time I saw him alive he was a full six feet from snout to tail. But winters were hard on him. He showed a tendency toward severe stiffness on cold mornings. When this happened Ed would draw Alligator out of his wooden pipe by the tail, heft him onto a shoulder like a carpenter toting a timber, and carry him inside to the fire.

Most of the customers in Scheller's Place became accustomed to sitting around the stove in cold weather with Alligator, all mummy-wrapped, lying at their feet waiting to thaw out.

"Sometimes," Ed said, a little sadness in his voice, "he'd lay there for weeks and never move."

Alligator was a benign beast and never bothered anybody even when thoroughly thawed. Oh, he did give a few of Ed's patrons a start a time or two when he showed sudden signs of thawing during a hot domino game. Ed said Alligator was just shifting, though. It gets tiresome sleeping in one position for a month.

Ed still can't explain why he neglected to bring Alligator inside the night that a really tight freeze hit the Texas coast. "I'll never forgive myself," he said.

The following morning Alligator was exceptionally stiff.

Tenderly, Ed extracted the beast from its box. Witnesses said he carried Alligator not shoulder-brace fashion but armlike, as a mother clutches a child to her breast. And he took the six-foot thing into his own home, and placed it by the fire.

Days passed. Weeks.

"I kept hoping he'd thaw out," Ed said, his voice quiet and hoarse. "But he never did."

And so Alligator passed on, to whatever reward might await a reptile.

CHAPTER 2

"I'm a magnetic healer . . . It's very interesting work."

— Hugo Weige, DST

A woman in a flowered sunbonnet came out of the red brick house to move the lawn sprinkler. She said the doctor was busy with a patient, but I could go in and take a seat and wait. Then she went off toward the barn.

In the town of Industry, nearly all the houses have barns behind them, and cow lots, and gardens. The doctor's house is different only in that it is red brick. The others are mostly white frame.

Dr. Hugo Weige's office is in a little building out back of his house. It's built of the same red brick. I went through the screen door, took a seat in the waiting room, and thumbed through the old farm magazines, trying without much success to get interested in articles about treating calves for screwworms and how many bales of cotton the flea hoppers and boll weevils destroy annually in the South.

For half an hour I listened to the muffled voices seeping out of the doctor's office in one end of the little building. Finally the patient emerged. A smiling middle-aged woman. The doctor followed and showed her to the door. Then he turned to me with a half-suspicious, inquiring expression, and I gave the little speech I had made up in advance. I told him I was interested in hearing exactly what kind of doctor he was, and about the nature of his work.

"I'm a magnetic healer," he said without hesitation, and stared me in the eye until he made me look away. "Let me get you one of my cards."

He ducked back into his office and got the card, a plain card not printed but typewritten. "H.W. Weige, DST," the card read. "Magnetic Healing and Absent Treatments. Industry, Texas."

I asked what, exactly, was magnetic healing.

"We treat people with our own personal magnetism," he said, using the editorial "we," for there is no other magnetic healer associated with him. "You've read in the Bible about the laying on of hands? Well, it's similar to that."

I guessed him to be up in his sixties. An average-built man. His eyes kept bothering me. His expression was pleasant but his eyes seemed to look inside and see private things. He was explaining about the magnetic healing. The human body, you know, is just full of electricity, he said, and when a patient comes to him he lays his hands on and the electricity from his own body enters that of the patient and passes through any defective parts and straightens them out.

I commented that it sounded like a fascinating idea, and the doctor said, "Yes, it's very interesting work."

The initials DST—what did they stand for?

"Doctor of Suggestive Therapy."

What about these absent treatments?

"That just means we treat people who aren't here."

Oh?

"Yes. We can treat a patient just by thinking about him, even though the patient is miles away. It's a concentrated thought force. We also treat a lot of livestock that way. Horses, cows, mules, ducks, dogs, just about anything."

For example, say you have a sick cow. So you leave the cow home and go to see Dr. Weige, and you describe the cow to him. She's a brown cow with white spots on her rump and shoulders, and she's muley. And her trouble is she coughs all the time and won't breed. So then the doctor summons up this cow in his vision and beams his concentrated thought force at her and treats her for the ailment. From that little red brick building there at Industry, Dr. Weige treats sick animals over a wide area. "Everything from scrubs to highbreds," he said.

While we talked a couple of cars drove up out front. Not old cars. New ones. Long black ones with white sidewalls. The doctor nodded his head toward the door and said that patients "from all over" come to him for the magnetic healing. A lot of people from Houston, about seventy-five miles east.

The absent-treatment idea really fascinated me, and the doctor gave me some case histories. He once sent his concentrated thought force all the way from Industry, Texas, to Newport, Rhode Island, to treat a sailor suffering with stomach ulcers. The sailor was bleeding to death, it seems, until a friend who knew Dr. Weige arranged for an absent treatment. "We stopped the bleeding," the doctor told me.

But even that wasn't a record for distance. Dr. Weige once treated a sick woman who was visiting over in Germany, and she was well by the time she got home.

How does the doctor account for this spectacular power he possesses?

"It's a God-given talent," he said. "I used to be an auto mechanic. One day I was over in La Grange being treated by a medical doctor and he told me, 'Anybody can fix cars. With your talent you ought to be healing people.'"

So Hugo Weige took a correspondence course, earned his DST, and opened an office. He never charges a nickel for his services. But if a patient wants to, now, he can leave a little something. Any amount he cares to leave.

"We never go out and make house calls," the doctor said. "We figure if a patient is unable to come here, then he needs a medical doctor. We have no argument with the medical profession."

He explained that the effectiveness of the magnetic treatments depends "on the cause of the trouble," that by laying on the hands he can determine whether the various organs are working right—the heart, the gall bladder, the kidneys, the stomach, and so on. He said if the patient really believes that a magnetic treatment can help him, then he can be helped.

Well, the door opened and two women came in to receive the smiling greeting from the magnetic healer. So I left, not wishing to delay their magnetic treatments.

I went back to see the doctor a couple of times after that, and we corresponded some, and I put him down in my book as a pretty remarkable fellow. I also determined, the next time I got sick, to give him a shot at curing me with an absent treatment. But months went by and I didn't get anything the matter with me, except for maybe a little headache and slight cases of nausea on Sunday mornings, and I didn't figure those were worth the effort it would take for the doctor to get his thought force concentrated and properly beamed.

But then our old tomcat got sick.

This tomcat, by the name of Figaro, had a pretty hairy reputation around our neighborhood. He had a good range and a lot of stamina, and half the weight he carried was scar tissue from wounds sustained in the course of his work. He even had fans who would come around to view him, because the word got about that his taste in rations was unique. That is, he liked squash and buttered asparagus and vegetable soup and chocolate ice cream. And Mentholatum. That's a fact. You rub Mentholatum on your chest

[33]

and he'd tear you up trying to get at it. Also he became pretty well known after he got shut up in the refrigerator and survived a night in there, and then he liked to wade around in the bathtub, too. So you can see that cat had character.

When he fell ill I drove to Industry and called on Dr. Weige. He was busy, as he generally is, and I spent half an hour studying the tractor ads in the farm magazines and debating myself on whether the doctor would mind being asked to treat a tomcat. I decided he wouldn't, since I had come to know him as a highly versatile citizen, and certainly not proud. Any doctor that will treat a Poland China sow for colic in the morning and a corporation president for ulcers in the afternoon oughtn't to mind doctoring a tomcat with character.

When the doctor dismissed his last patient, he came smiling out of his chambers with that cordial greeting, and we passed the time of day for a while, discussing such matters as how things are in the magnetic-healing profession, and he said things were just fine.

So then I brought up the matter of the tomcat, explaining that his illness was of serious concern to the juveniles around my house, as well as to a number of the tomcat's fans.

"A shame," Dr. Weige said, in a sympathetic tone that a lot of M.D.s would do well to use. "Children do love cats. Well, we will work on him. Let me get my paper."

He disappeared for a second and returned with a pencil and pad. "Now what seems to be his trouble?"

Well, Doctor, to begin with, he has suffered a total loss of appetite and has dropped about six of his normal fourteen pounds. And he is completely listless, with a dullness in his eyes and a tendency to stay indoors at night—highly unusual for this time of year, since spring is his busy season.

Dr. Weige nodded, his face calm and professional, his hand flying across the writing pad. "What is his color?"

He is gray, Doctor, and brindle.

"Gray . . . brindle," repeated the doctor, writing it down. He also took various other of the cat's statistics, including his name. It seems the name is necessary. Possibly the doctor meant to call it when he summoned up our tomcat in his vision and sent his thought waves zipping out to find old Figaro no matter where he was. Even, I assumed, if he was in the refrigerator again.

"We will treat him for appetite," the doctor said, rising and looking over his notes, "and also for worms. You should notice some improvement in a day or two. These absent treatments are a wonderful thing. We are treating some people in England now."

As I left he added, "And don't worry. The cat's going to be all right."

Thus assured, I went my way and Dr. Weige returned to his chambers, presumably to get busy giving absent treatments, since no patients were on hand in person.

Now. I want to say I didn't take the sick cat case to Dr. Weige to test him. I never test people, mostly I guess out of fear they will test me in return. All I know about Hugo Weige, DST, is that he has an awful lot of satisfied patients, and that he is an interesting, mysterious man.

But about the tomcat.

Within twenty-four hours that cat was able to sit up and take some light broth. Within forty-eight hours he had returned to full rations. Within three days he again went forth to make his rounds—the fire in his eye and that old snap back in his step.

Two years later, in a veterinary hospital, he died of internal complications developing from wounds suffered fighting for what he thought was right. And we buried him out by the woodpile, in soft brown earth moistened by a shower of tears.

I'll always wonder if another absent treatment might have saved him.

Industry, Hugo Weige's town, is in the heart of the Texas German country in Austin County. Just north lies Washington County.

When the Germans immigrated to this region, they brought with them some of the best brains Texas has today. A few also brought strange talents.

One sunny morning I was strolling around the Washington County Courthouse square, in Brenham, and spotted a fellow of about thirty cutting a branch off a peach tree that grows on the courthouse lawn. He put the branch in his car and drove off. It stirs up my curiosity to see things like that, and I went in the courthouse and asked about it. The man, I was told, owns a farm a few miles outside town. He is a good farmer and stockman, with a degree from one of Texas's leading agricultural colleges. Why would he be snipping branches off a tree on the courthouse lawn?

"Oh, my guess would be he's fixing to drill him a water well," my informant said, "and is gonna use the switch to witch with. I'd say better than half the new wells in this county even today are witched up before they're drilled."

Well, of course everybody has heard of water witching, or dowsing or divining, but I had the notion it was an old superstition long dead. We used to play at water witching with forked sticks when we were kids. But if college graduates were using switches to locate underground water . . . I inquired around and got the name of a man said to be the best water witcher in Washington County.

I found Fritz Kroehler sitting on the front porch of his farmhouse a few miles east of Brenham. He said he'd be glad to give me a demonstration on how to witch a water well if I'd go down yonder in the borrow ditch and cut him a first-growth willow switch.

Some Texas water witchers use a forked limb off a peach tree. Some use a straight switch. Some say it doesn't matter what kind of wood they use or whether the switch is forked or not. A few use a Bible, with a string hanging out of it and a key tied on the end. Kroehler prefers a straight willow switch.

"It's got to be first-growth willow, now," he cautioned as I walked with his son Norris down the highway where the willow was growing in the ditch. "New growth off an old willow is no good, either. Make it about two and a half feet long."

Norris Kroehler had brought a hatchet and hacked us a path through the poison oak that grew around the willow sprouts in the ditch.

"Lot of folks don't believe in this witching," he said. "But Dad has found a lot of water this way. Now it won't work for me." He laughed a little. "Maybe I'm not concentrating. It works for my sister, though."

We took the stick back to Kroehler and he trimmed it up with his pocketknife, walked to a bare spot in his front yard, and squatted down. "It won't work where there's grass," he said. "I don't know if there's any water right here, but we'll give her a try."

Squatting there, he explained just what the switch would tell him.

"If there's water below, the switch will dip for every foot of depth to the water. If it dips twenty times, you'll want to drill your well twenty feet deep. If it's a strong vein of water the switch will move fast and you really have to count quick to keep up. If the vein's weak, she'll move slow. If there's solid rock down there, the switch'll move from side to side instead of up and down."

Now Kroehler sat down on his shoes, with knees together in front of him. He laid the switch on the bare ground and waited a few seconds, like a circus performer pauses, balanced, to await the precise moment before turning a backward flip on a tight wire.

Norris Kroehler and I stood silent and respectful. Cars whizzed by on the highway, and I wondered what the people in them thought.

Kroehler picked up the switch, held it in tightly clenched fists. He braced his fists firmly between his knees. "So I won't move my hands," he said quietly. When in position the switch was held up at an angle of about forty-five degrees, the heavier end out.

It didn't move.

"If there's no water there," Kroehler said, relaxing, "you can bet she won't move."

He went out back of the house where he knew there was water, because his well was there. He'd witched it up long ago. He assumed the position near the well. "You watch, now," he said, "and see if you can tell me how deep it is to water."

The switch moved. It bobbed up and down, pretty fast. I counted eighteen bobs.

"That's right," said Kroehler, smiling at me. "Eighteen feet to water."

I wasn't certain what that proved, but followed Kroehler down in his pasture. He said the water table was high there and that he knew a spot where water lay just ten feet below ground. He worked the switch at the spot. It dipped ten times, and I asked if I could have a go at it. Sure, Kroehler said.

[38]

So I got down in the proper position, there in Fritz Kroehler's pasture with a bull and six mother cows as witnesses, and tried to witch a little water. I felt like a fool. The stick wouldn't move for me.

Kroehler laughed. "Well, it works for some and for some it doesn't. Now my daughter, lives down in Galveston, not long ago she witched a hundred-foot well."

I thanked my host for the demonstration, accepted the switch as a souvenir of the visit, drove home, and got out the encyclopedia.

It pleased me to discover that Mr. Britannica devotes forty-seven lines of small type to a straight-faced discussion of the dowser and the use of the divining rod. The practice got started back in the fifteenth century in the Harz Mountains of Germany, a mining area. The early German dowsers used forked sticks to look for minerals, and taught the technique to traveling British merchants of Queen Elizabeth's day. A lot of dowsing was done in the Cornwall mines. When Cornish minerals played out, dowsers used forked sticks and a variety of other contrivances to search for underground water.

The water-witching business stayed under my hide for months. Was Fritz Kroehler pulling my leg? Did the willow switch really move in his hands? If he made it move, consciously, he did a good job of concealing the trick.

There once lived a British professor, Sir W. F. Barrett, who made thorough investigations into dowsing and became satisfied that the divining rod does indeed move without any conscious effort on the part of the dowser. The good professor felt this is due to what he called the dowser's motor automatism. This in turn is described as reflex action set off by a stimulus that the encyclopedia didn't quite manage to explain in terms I could understand.

What it boiled down to was that dowsing is all a mighty mysterious phenomenon, which I already knew.

Within the year after my visit with Fritz Kroehler I met a few more water witchers, most of whom didn't do much talking. Floyd O'Pry talked, though, and told me about the time he discovered he had the gift.

I looked for O'Pry well outside the German country. My directions said to drive to Ratcliff Lake, up in the Piney Woods of Houston County, and look for a buckskin mare named Molly tethered to a sapling. O'Pry wouldn't be far away.

Now there is a lovely set of directions. Molly was easy to find. She stood sound asleep with her muzzle almost resting on the bark of a pine sapling. I sat down nearby and waited. The directions said Molly single-foots her master the three miles from his house to the lake just about every day of the week so O'Pry can fish for black bass and white perch.

In about fifteen minutes a man came paddling across the lake in a skiff. I knew it was O'Pry because Molly woke up and aimed her ears at the boat. When he beached the skiff, I guessed O'Pry to be in his middle seventies. A small man. Sharp features. Gold-rimmed glasses. Wore a brown felt hat pulled way down in front, so he had to cock his head and look up when he talked.

"I'm what they call a natural geologist," he said when we sat down under the pines. Molly wasn't pleased I'd delayed her master. She stomped and tossed her head and switched her tail and pretended flies were bothering her. She was thinking about that bucket of crimped oats waiting back home, I expect.

"I can locate water underground, and metals, and I think I can locate oil, too," O'Pry was saying. "I use a straight stick. Any kind'll do long as it's got plenty sap. See this gold watch? If I lost this watch out here, I'd get me a switch and split the end of it and put a piece of gold in it and I could find the watch."

Pretending I'd never heard of such a marvel, I asked O'Pry how he accounted for this astounding ability.

"Don't you ever read the Bible?" he scolded. "The Bible says the gifts of God are without repentance. It's a gift I have."

So I asked him to tell me how he discovered the gift. It was a question I hadn't got answered from the other dowsers I'd met. O'Pry was eager to answer it.

"Well, it was after I was up and married and had a family. We needed a new water well. I'd heard about this water-witching stuff, and the truth is I didn't really believe in it. But I got me a peach limb and just started playin' around with it.

"I walked in front of the house, holding the limb out, and went around the corner of the porch. All of a sudden my switch turned on me. I backed up and walked around the porch a second time and she turned again. I said to myself, I bet I can get by there without that switch turning. Well, I backed up and tried again. But she turned anyway. I couldn't *keep* it from turning. I didn't know what to think.

"But I got me some help and started digging and it was just twelve feet to water. Just twelve feet. By dinner that day we drank clear water out of that well."

This experience decided O'Pry's career. All his working life he was a locator and a digger of water wells. He dug just by golly and by gosh, using a shovel and a drive shaft out of a Model T Ford for a drill. By the time he retired and he and Molly took up fishing, he was charging two dollars a foot to dig wells.

I had not met a dowser who claimed he could locate metal with a divining rod. I dug in my pocket and came

[41]

up with a twenty-five-cent piece. If I lost that quarter there on the lake bank, could O'Pry find it with a sappy stick?

"Let me get a switch," he said, and walked about fifty yards down the waterline, pausing a minute to speak a few quiet words to Molly. He came back whittling on a slender willow switch about a foot and a half long. He split the end of it, took a quarter out of his own pocket, and inserted the coin in the split.

Then he took my quarter and tossed it off to one side, no more than ten feet. It disappeared into a litter of pine needles.

Now O'Pry stood motionless, pausing prior to the performance in that same way Fritz Kroehler had done. He held the switch straight up in front of him, with the quarter not six inches from the end of his nose. The switch then began to make a nodding motion, as a person's head might nod to indicate a direction. O'Pry walked slowly in the direction of the nod. He took five, maybe six steps. The switch stopped nodding. The end of it then began to rotate slowly, sending the quarter in circles. "That's the way it does when you're over the metal," O'Pry said. He stooped down, picked up the quarter, and looked at me with an expression that said, "Now what do you think of that?"

What I thought was that it wasn't too impressive a performance. I felt I could have found the quarter by getting down on my hands and knees and rummaging through the pine needles. I started to mention this, but O'Pry had tossed the quarter again, almost at my feet, and was offering to let me try the switch.

Of course it wouldn't move for me.

"Now let me put my hands on yours," O'Pry said, "and maybe you can feel it move." So there on the shore of Ratcliff Lake, with the jay birds laughing at us from the trees and Molly the buckskin mare looking on with contempt, Floyd O'Pry and I stood over a twenty-five-cent piece holding a willow switch. He clasped his hands around mine. The stick nodded toward the quarter.

I could feel movement in O'Pry's hands, all right. But was he moving them purposely, or was the stick causing them to move? Or was he moving them unconsciously, via his motor automatism, as Professor Barrett said?

I couldn't tell. But I am certain that O'Pry thought the stick moved on its own, just as Kroehler and the others did, and perhaps that's the significant thing.

I discovered that I fell the victim of my own investigation into dowsing. When O'Pry agreed to locate the tossed quarter and went off to get his stick, I planned to heave the coin twenty-five or thirty yards up the lake bank into the bushes and give the willow switch a tough test.

But I didn't. I waited and let O'Pry toss the quarter, and he gave it a mighty small toss. Driving home, I finally admitted to myself that I wanted so strongly to believe in the dowsing stick that I hesitated to throw the coin very far. Because O'Pry might not have been able to find it, and of course that would have ruined everything.

Maybe I ought not to tell this. Likely it will mark me as an awful sucker for a legend and a mystery. But then I suppose a guy that will drive over half of Texas watching water witchers wave their sticks is not getting out of character when he stands on a riverbank and tries to hear a dead man play a fiddle.

I had just about recovered from my siege of curiosity about the water witchers when somebody offered me a set of directions on how to find Fiddler's Island. The directions said to go first to Charlie Ducroz's house and get there early or else Ducroz would be off down the river seeing after his cows.

I got there maybe a little too early. Ducroz was still sitting in his wife's spotless kitchen drinking coffee—coffee with a fertile aroma that might remind you of that dark brew they served you the time you drove down Louisiana 308 below New Orleans and stopped for a cup, say, at Lafourche.

There are a great many authorities in the San Bernard River Bottom on the Legend of Fiddler's Island. There are still others that talk of the legend in the barbershops and beer joints of such towns as Bay City, Freeport, and Angleton. But Charlie Ducroz is likely the best living authority on the legend. He inherited this position.

Still, he is a reluctant authority. Reluctant, I think, because the barbershop and beer joint talk has embellished the legend over the years and got it all out of shape. Ducroz is a man that has a high regard for a fact and wouldn't create a detail out of his imagination just for the sake of keeping a tall story in circulation.

So when Ducroz says he has listened many times to the mysterious music around Fiddler's Island, you know he isn't just spoofing the tourists. What he knows about the island came from his parents and his grandparents, who were among the early settlers on the San Bernard in Brazoria County. Ducroz lives now a few miles above that quiet stream's mouth, so close to the river he can step out his back door, flip a match, and hit water.

"The story," he said, there in his wife's kitchen, "was that in the early days around here a man and his wife were on the river in a bateau, a little square-ended boat. The man was a musician, a fiddler.

"Now about four miles downriver from here there used to be a channel called The Narrows. That's where Fiddler's

[44]

Island is. It was the narrowest spot on the San Bernard. There was a shell reef at that spot, and the current was real swift. Well, the fiddler and his wife got into that current and the bateau turned upside down and they both drowned."

So that's how the story began. The legend says that for years afterward, when the weather was right, you could hear the fiddler still playing his music around the island and at times even several miles upstream from the spot where he and his wife drowned.

Which wouldn't be such a hot legend except that just a mighty lot of people have heard this music. Charlie Ducroz has heard it many times. He doesn't know what makes the sound, and it's doubtful that any man has had a better opportunity to study and analyze it.

"The last time I heard it must have been twenty-five years ago," Ducroz told me. "I was sitting in a skiff right near here, not down at The Narrows. It was about sundown."

Did the noise sound like fiddle music?

"Well, you might say it did, some. But it was more like a hum, or a buzz. Like an old bumblebee."

Ducroz said the noise itself is not as mysterious as the way it behaves. He and various others who have heard the sound on the river say it does a lot of moving around.

"It'll start off like it's just ten feet over your head, and then move off across the river, and then come back and hum all around you, and then trail off again. I used to bump the side of the boat with the paddle when the noise was around me, and the sound would go away real sudden. Then maybe it'd come back again."

Ducroz's factual appraisal of the mystery wouldn't go over any too well around the barbershops and beer joints, where the ear witnesses say they can still hear the noise (at midnight, of course, when the wind is still) and that it sounds so much like fiddle music that a man can almost recognize the tune. That's the way, of course, legends are supposed to be.

I tried to get Ducroz to theorize on exactly what makes the noise.

"I don't know," he said. "They used to say it was caused by the current over the shell reef. And it's true I didn't hear it as often after they started dredging shell out of The Narrows. Still I heard it a long way upriver from that reef. Then some used to say it was caused by a fish. I just don't know."

Whatever caused it, the noise is, or was, there and has fascinated or frightened three generations of people along the San Bernard.

The conditions were wrong, because it wasn't a still evening and it wasn't midnight, but I drove down the river road to Fiddler's Island determined to listen for the music.

The island itself is a pitiful piece of dirt. It sits low and small and reedy in the river near where the stream empties into the Gulf. There wasn't any fiddle music.

I went back to Fiddler's Island twice after that. I've never told anybody about it because it seemed even then a foolish effort, especially since Charlie Ducroz said he hadn't heard the music in a quarter century. But one of the barbershop-beer joint boys swore, over a bottle he clutched in his hand (with three or four empties at his elbow) that he'd heard the music not a month before as he was coming up the river road from a fishing trip. After midnight.

The first time I went back the weather kicked up and there wasn't anything to hear but the wind.

The last time, almost a year after I talked with Ducroz, conditions were perfect. It's a lonesome drive down that river road at midnight. What strange things a man will do in search of the mysterious.

[46]

So finally I got to stand on the bank of the San Bernard, at midnight, with the weather calm and the moon shining, and listen for the music on Fiddler's Island while the river slipped silently by.

A dog barked far across the marsh. A fish jumped in the river. A night bird swished along overhead. The current whispered around the island's head. No other sounds.

I stayed half an hour and got cold. Then a man's loud belly laugh floated up from one of the fish camps downstream, faint but clear. I detected derision in that laugh, and got in the car and drove off. I haven't been back.

CHAPTER 3

"I can remember my daddy gettin' up at two o'clock
in the morning, buildin' a fire in the stove and fid-
dlin' until daylight."

—Ross Foley

About an hour before sunset I found Drayton Speights relaxing in the front yard of his comfortable country home
on Palo Gaucho Creek. His house stands a few miles north of
Hemphill, in Sabine County near the Texas-Louisiana line.

Speights is old enough to have grandchildren, and a couple of them were playing around the yard. By the front
porch a huge wisteria in heavy bloom was breathing its
perfume over the premises and on account of those flowers
the wisteria was working alive with big black bumblebees.
Speights's grandchildren—just little ones maybe not school
age yet—were ducking in and out and around and under
that wisteria and the bumblebees were zooming around
their ears, and I remarked to Speights that, if I were to
stick my head in that shrub the way those children were
doing, I'd be stung sick.

"Why, those bees won't sting," Speights said, apparently
surprised at my ignorance. "Let me show you." He rose from
his lawn chair, stepped to the wisteria, and with his bare
hand he grabbed the biggest, ugliest bumblebee he could
locate.

"Notice this bee's head," Speights said, returning to his
chair with the bee trapped between his thumb and fore-

[48]

finger. "It's got a white spot on it. A bumblebee with a white face like this *can't* sting. Now the black-faced bee, he'll sting you, but this is a different species."

He held the buzzing insect out, as if he expected me to take it. I declined, for several reasons.

One was that when I was a good bit older than Speights's grandchildren I came home to supper more than once with both eyes swollen shut from bumblebee stings. Fighting bumblebees was considered a necessary sport in my bare-foot and overalled days. By necessary I mean that I never really enjoyed fighting the things and I suspect now that my associates didn't either, but it was something we did to show that we weren't afraid to, just the same as we jumped off the top of the barn into a pile of hay and chided those who wouldn't do it. The brand of bumblebees we fought (I never thought to inspect their faces for white spots) had a nasty habit of searching out the eyes, and loved to pop you square on the bridge of the nose so you'd look like a punch-drunk boxer when you got home. The puffier you swelled the more your fellow bee fighters laughed, and you were supposed to grin and say "Naw" when asked if the stings were hurting. They hurt, all right.

Did you ever ride along a country road in a wagon when you were young and play the bumblebee game? When the wagon passed within reaching distance of tall sunflowers you were supposed to reach out and grab a bloom and snap it off in your fist. The idea was to try to get one that didn't have a bumblebee in it. If you grabbed a bee, you'd be lying in bed late that night, throbbing from fingernails to armpits.

A foolish game, yes, and I am through with foolish games, so I didn't care to accept that bumblebee offered by Drayton Speights. But there was another reason. Speights is one of these citizens who like to play pranks on people. On account of his reputation, if he were to offer me a monarch butterfly I wouldn't take it for fear he'd have the thing rigged up some way with a stinger.

People around Sabine County tell you they threw the mold away after they made Drayton Speights. That's not quite right. The fact is at least every county and most all communities in rural Texas have a guy of Speights's pattern around, spicing up an existence that might otherwise be pretty uneventful. Such guys will devote an unbelievable amount of planning and labor to pulling a caper that everybody (save the victims) will get a kick out of. Maybe you are among that multitude which believes the world would be better off without the practical joker. Well, I think men like Speights serve a useful purpose, at least in a country town.

A practical joker around an office in a city is now apt to be held in thorough contempt. Not so in the country. I think the practical joke ranks near the top as an entertainment medium in rural Texas. Its purpose is not to ridicule but to test. If a man is able to grin and bear up when victimized, then he is considered a regular fellow who is worth victimizing. If he stays peeved about it, his stock goes down. I don't think a fellow like Drayton Speights would waste his time planning a stunt on a man he didn't like.

Speights is a big fellow who talks slow and dry and straight and doesn't smile much except with his eyes. He is described as just a guy that knows everybody and everything that goes on around Sabine County. He's been in local politics, and he runs a few cows there along Palo Gaucho Creek. His greatest achievement was the Flying Saucer of the Sabine, though he also turned a vicious female lion loose in that region once and even invented an oil boom, with a typewriter and a piece of onionskin paper.

"It was just after the war, about 1945," Speights told me that spring afternoon, sitting there holding the bumblebee in his hand. "We had a doctor here then whose wife had a Slavic background. She spoke that language. Czechoslovakian, I guess it was. And she carried on some correspondence with people in Europe. Then there's a fella here named Parker. Tom Parker. Retired now. Had a drugstore in Hemphill. He used to play croquet with several of the men around town, three, four nights a week.

"Well, that was when the flying saucers were in the news, and one day I got to talking with Parker about 'em, about whether or not such a thing existed. So I told him if he'd let me know where they were gonna play croquet next, I'd have a flying saucer made up and we'd let the croquet players have a look at it. So I got a garageman to make the thing. It was metal, about four or five feet across. Looked about like a chick brooder.

"We put some old radio tubes and wire and things inside it, and I got a letter from this doctor's wife, written in that foreign language. One she'd really received from over in Europe. When the saucer was finished I got Parker to put me up to where the bunch was playing croquet. They played at night on lighted courts, and they moved around from house to house. So the next night they played I put the saucer in the lane, a private road that ran up to the house where the game was. It was a narrow lane and the saucer was wide enough you couldn't drive around it. For a long time I stayed around there in the bushes waiting for the game to break up, but it kept holding out and I got sleepy and went on home to bed."

Rising early the following morning and going into town, Speights found the little city of Hemphill in a big stir. The local newspaper, a weekly, had been printed the night before. It sported a banner headline announcing that a flying saucer had been found in Sabine County. The word had spread. Newspaper and radio reporters from Shreveport and Beaumont had arrived to view the saucer and send their stories out. The sheriff had hauled the saucer into town to the courthouse.

It had been late when the saucer was discovered. The croquet players, Speights learned, wouldn't touch it. One got a shovel and pushed it off in the ditch to clear the road. The sheriff was summoned.

"A lot of people came into town that morning to see the thing," Speights said. "I had rolled up the letter I got from the doctor's wife and put it in a glass vial and stuck it up inside the saucer. When the vial was found, somebody said it oughtn't to be opened by hand because it might be booby-trapped and explode. So one fellow took the vial and threw it against a wall of the courthouse." Speights grinned a little for the first time. "That way, you know, if the thing exploded, all it'd do would be blow up our courthouse. They finally got the letter out but it was written in this foreign language and nobody could read it."

The hoax was slow dying. For more than a week Speights had the boundless pleasure of standing around listening to people speculate about his flying saucer. A local grocer had the sheriff carry the saucer to his store, where it stayed on display for days. People would poke around it, examine the thing, guess whether it was constructed in such a way that it would really fly. Some thought it wouldn't, some thought it would.

At last a Hemphill attorney who knew something about languages dealt the death thrust to the flying saucer. He discovered that the letter was written in Czech and not in the mysterious language of another planet. Speights said he doesn't know what ever happened to the saucer.

In the end it was the grocer who benefited the most.

When he displayed the saucer his trade boomed. Tom Parker, the druggist who was in on the hoax, tried to get the saucer and park it in front of his store, seeing it was such a drawing card. But the grocer wouldn't give it up.

The saucer was Speights's masterpiece, but the oil boom he created lasted longer.

If you've never lived in oil country, maybe you don't know how a wildcat well in the process of drilling can inspire some marvelous fiction. Most wildcats are drilled tight, which is an oilman's way of saying that no information is being put out about what the drill bit has or hasn't discovered. But a community badly in need of the economic benefits that accompany the discovery of a new oil field just refuses to sit around and wait for official information.

When the hole nears the depth to which it is originally scheduled, stories begin circulating. You hear them on every corner, at every crossroads. Half the county is floating on one of the biggest oil fields ever discovered. The company that drilled the well is not putting out any information until it can block up leases and sew up the productive area. Why, you can go out there and even see oil floating around on top of the slush pit. (Even though that may be nothing more than lubricating oil that leaked out of the rig's draw works.) Sam Such-and-such, on whose land the well is being drilled, is flat a millionaire now, but he's being quiet about it. Wouldn't you? Joe So-and-so, his land starts not two hundred feet from the drill site, got a bonus of a thousand dollars an acre to sign a mineral lease. Jim Whatziz, his cousin's a geologist in Houston, you know, said he heard from a friend of this cousin who's an oil scout that the well had tested out two thousand barrels a day.

Now the chances are better than good that these stories are nothing but yarns, but they always circulate when a tight wildcat is being drilled. People want to believe them. Small-town businessmen say that such rumors may improve their business by respectable percentages. Even the suggestion of a boom, the rare possibility, makes people act as if they suddenly have more money to spend than they did a month before.

So you can see why, when a wildcat began drilling near Hemphill, citizens of Sabine County were anxious for information. It happens everywhere. Drayton Speights knew this.

He took a piece of official-looking onionskin paper and typed off a letter. Made it look like a carbon copy of a report from a certain geophysical firm, informing the company drilling the well of what a core test had shown. One day somebody found this important-looking report lying on the floor of the Hemphill Post Office, where, obviously, it had been dropped. The news circulated. The report said that the bit had penetrated at four thousand feet a thick and porous and fully saturated formation.

Well, there it was, in black and white. An oil strike for Sabine County. It took the excitement, and all the benefits and disadvantages that go along with the prospect of an oil boom, about two weeks to die out. And I don't doubt that there are those in Sabine County who believe to this day that the company that drilled that well did find oil there but capped it off and refused to produce it and thus deprived the region of a boom. Oil companies are always getting accused of that, anyway.

Speights's female lion lasted a good deal longer than his oil boom.

He didn't even invent the lion. Somebody else started the rumor, that a lion had been seen roaming the woods around Brookeland, a little Piney Woods community in lower Sabine County. Knowing a setup when he heard it,

Speights went back to work with his typewriter. He wrote a letter to one of his friends in Hemphill and signed it as Fritz Dobrinsky, director of the Dallas County Zoo. The letter said that the animal being seen at Brookeland was doubtless a female lion recently escaped from the zoo in Dallas. It also said that the animal likely had two cubs, since she was expecting when she escaped, and therefore she was extraordinarily dangerous.

A couple of lion hunts were organized. People began seeing things.

"I had perfectly reliable people," Speights said, "who'd never told a lie in all their life tell me that they'd seen the lion's tracks and heard it roar. Why, they lost a whole blackberry crop down there that spring because everybody was afraid to go out and pick 'em."

A game warden finally punctured the lion scare by investigating and announcing that the Dallas County Zoo did not exist.

But you can see why a guy wouldn't want to take in his hand a bumblebee Drayton Speights offered him, no matter whether it had a white face or not. Still, I suppose it was an authentic lesson in entomology he was giving me, because after I declined to handle the bumblebee one of Speights's grandchildren came up and asked if he could have it, and his grandfather handed it to him.

It isn't just Sabine County people who're willing to believe wild animal stories. The folk history of rural Texas is replete with accounts of lion and tiger and gorilla yarns invented by men of imagination and purpose.

The best one I ever ran down concerned Ben Myatt's lion in Robertson County. It's one of the few lion hoaxes in which the perpetrator ever really got his comeuppance in the end, and it gave an entire county a nickname.

I found Ben Myatt, after a considerable search, living in a garage apartment in Groesbeck. He was willing to tell all, confess the whole business. Myatt is a friendly, grinning gent who loves bird dogs and guns and fishing and hunting. A good storyteller.

"It was the first year of national Prohibition," he began, "and I was spending a lot of my time camped on a hunting lease along the Brazos River in Robertson County a few miles out of Bremond. When Prohibition came along a lot of people in that part of the country took to moonshining. They used to come on my lease and hide their mash. The lease was grown up in thickets and made a good place to hide a barrel. Well, every couple days they'd go out to check their mash and they'd take along their guns, pretending to hunt, you know, and a lot of 'em got to pot-shootin' my quail. Out of season, too."

So that's why Myatt invented the lion, which had escaped from a circus. He spread the word that the beast was prowling his lease. He hoped this would keep the moonshiners from harvesting his birds. Not so many believed the story until they began hearing the lion roar.

The roar was produced by a contrivance that Myatt made and referred to as a "dumb bull." He stretched a rawhide over a wooden form, a sort of long, rectangular pipe or column. To the rawhide he attached a resin-powdered string. When Myatt's hand slid down this string, the rawhide echoed down the wooden pipe and produced a fierce noise similar to a lion's roar.

Myatt hid in a thicket with his lion-roaring machine and waited. A man finally came along the lane in a buggy. Myatt slid his hand along the string and was astonished at the result. The fellow took off to town and spread the news of his experience.

"He told people he not only heard the lion but saw it,

and that the thing chased him," Myatt recalled. "He said the only reason it didn't catch him was that its head was too big to go through the fence."

The first victim's experience set the countryside to seething. Many heard the lion roar on successive nights and few were courageous enough to venture into the thickets to check their mash. Myatt could sit on a log and produce the roar, and shotguns up to a mile away would blast wildly into the night.

"One bootlegger," Myatt recalls, grinning, "claims he was treed on top of his own house all night long by that lion, and he told everybody he wounded it."

Some considered that the roar wasn't produced by a lion at all but by a devil, come from underground to punish the wicked. Others called it a "bugger," an old expression used in reference to a ghost or an unknown thing. Robertson County is today still called "Bugger County," and Myatt insists that his lion inspired the nickname.

The lion scare eventually got a little out of hand. A country school and a church were closed up because women and children feared to walk abroad.

"I didn't mind about the men so much," Myatt said. "They needed something to keep them home at night. But I hated to scare the women and children."

A hunt was planned. Myatt said it was the biggest mass hunt ever held on the Brazos. Scores and scores of men carrying every weapon available got together and combed the thickets along the river in search of the roaring beast.

"On the Saturday before the hunt," Myatt said, "every store in Bremond sold out of ammunition, and some were buying knives."

After the hunt was over, Ben Myatt looked around him and decided the brunt of the joke fell on himself. Searching for a lion that didn't exist, the hunters burned off about fifteen hundred acres of Myatt's thickets and ran every last quail off his hunting lease.

Ross Foley was sitting among some old oil cans in his filling station at Jewett the afternoon I sought him out to talk about country music. He stopped what he was doing immediately, reached for a battered black case, and carefully drew out of it an ancient fiddle.

"No, sir," he said, lightly thumbing the strings, "there's not enough money in that Jewett bank to buy this fiddle. It belonged to my daddy, Uncle Tom Foley, and it was given to him by Bob Wills."

Uncle Tom Foley has been dead since 1957, but in the world of what fiddlers and guitar pickers refer to as Texas breakdown music, Uncle Tom's name won't ever fade. He was champion fiddler of Texas for fifteen years and seldom came out second best in a contest.

"When Bob Wills was just a youngster," Foley said, taking his father's old bow out of the case, "my daddy gave him the first fiddle he ever owned. Bob's mother and my daddy were brother and sister. Bob was born over at Kosse, I think it was, but the Willses lived out here about ten miles in the country till Bob was a big kid and then they moved to Memphis."

While he talked, Ross drew Uncle Tom's bow experimentally across the fiddle strings. "Well, after Bob had made good in country and western music, along about in the late 1920s he came to my daddy and he said, 'Uncle Tom, you gave me my first fiddle, and you helped me and I want to do something for you.' So he gave him this very fiddle. What it's worth I wouldn't guess. I figure it must be over a hundred years old."

There was a honk out on the driveway of the filling station. A customer had driven in and Foley hadn't noticed. He called out the front door, "Just help yourself to whatever you want. I'm kind of busy now."

So while the customer helped himself to a tank of gas, Ross Foley set his foot to patting and the bow to sawing, and out came a nice chorus of "Leather Britches." And then some of "Take Me Back to Texas" and a bit of "Tom and Jerry," the tune Uncle Tom Foley played to win so many of his contests.

I looked down and saw my own foot patting and my pencil keeping time on the edge of the notebook. A funny thing, I never was very high on country and western and breakdown music. I always preferred something I considered more sophisticated, and I ran around Texas for years before I paid much attention to the great influence that fiddle music has on country and small-town Texans. It has to rank as the true folk music of Texas, the music of the great majority of the people. Sure, in Houston and Dallas there are thousands who dance to popular music and dress up and attend symphony concerts, and likely these people would snort at the idea that country music is the music of the people of this state. But they just haven't ever driven down a highway on Saturday night and counted the country dance spots, crowded to the rafters with people lured out by fiddle sawing and guitar picking. I'd bet that among Texans who take an active interest in music, there are ten country and western fans to each person who prefers popular or classical fare. I can't prove that. I just bet that way.

I discovered you can't appreciate country music just by listening to it on radio or television. You've got to be there, where it's being produced, and sit and watch as well as listen. I learned the same thing about Mexican music. Thousands of Texans have a grudge against Mexican music because they grew up in those years when the best available entertainment consisted of listening to Amos 'n' Andy and Fibber McGee and Molly on radio. About the time Fibber would open his closet and you'd lean close to the speaker to hear all the contents spill out in that grand and noisy way, your station would fade and get overpowered by some Mexican signal. And instead of hearing Fibber's closet empty itself you'd hear a bunch of Mexicans singing and guitaring and spitting out words so fast you couldn't understand them even if you made A in textbook Spanish.

I really hated the sound of Mexican singers until I started going to Mexico. Then a friend who lives down there taught me that just listening to Mexican singers, as on radio or a record, is something different from watching them sing. It's the difference between bitter and sweet. I've ended up a nut about mariachi bands, and when I go to Mexico I spend many more pesos than are prudent hiring them to sing. It's the same music I used to cuss in the Fibber McGee days.

The tunes Ross Foley played in his filling station that day were also the ones I used to sneer at, along with all my high-school associates, when we thought the only music worth listening to was played by Tommy Dorsey and Glenn Miller.

But if you can sit there in Foley's service station, or anywhere else, and watch him saw away at "Leather Britches" and "Take Me Back to Texas" and fail to pat your foot, then you were born with a stone ear. That's when you learn about country music, and why so many people love it and why it's such a great part of the entertainment of rural people.

Country music has a way of becoming family tradition, and families often take pride in the fact that all the members are musical. The Foleys at Jewett are this way. Uncle Tom Foley had three brothers, all musicians. There was Blue-Eye Foley, whose first name was George but who went by the nickname because he had one blue eye and one brown, and there was Uncle Jim Foley, then Feely Foley, all fiddlers.

It's difficult for an outsider to grasp the hold that music has on true country entertainers. "You know," Ross Foley said, finishing his fiddling there in the filling station, "I can remember my daddy getting up at two o'clock in the morning, building a fire in the stove and fiddlin' until daylight, whether there was anybody listening or not." He laid the old fiddle reverently back in its case. "Music was just in him," Ross said, "and it had to come out."

A friend called me one night and said Tex Owens had moved back to his native state from California and was living on a farm near New Baden, not far from where Ross Foley played in the filling station. A few days later we drove up to Owens' front door just as dusk was settling over the post oak, and Tex showed us into his comfortable living room. He wasn't in first-class health then, but his big rangy frame still looked strong for the seventy years it carried. His face showed that curious quality of clean ruggedness that seems to say here's a man that's led a hardworking and upright life. I wanted to meet Owens to see if he'd talk about how he wrote "Cattle Call," one of this nation's greatest Western songs.

"It was a winter morning in 1933," Tex said, "and I was sitting in an office building on the eleventh floor of the Pickwick Hotel in Kansas City, where the studios of KCBM were. Well, snow began falling. Small flakes at first, then big ones, so thick it blotted out my view of the buildings through the window. Now I grew up on a ranch, and I used to do a lot of cattle feeding and in winter I could never help feeling sorry for all the dumb animals out in the wet and cold.

"Well, sittin' there in the hotel, watchin' that snow, my sympathy went out to cattle everywhere, and I just wished I could call 'em all around me and break some corn over a wagon wheel and feed 'em. That's when the words 'cattle call' came to my mind. I picked up my guitar and in thirty minutes I'd written the music and words—four verses—to 'Cattle Call.'"

The mournful yodeling chorus of that song is now considered a true classic by lovers of Western music. Eddy Arnold adopted it as a theme, and uses it today. It was one of more than a hundred sixty songs that Tex Owens composed, and royalties from these tunes still come in to that little farmhouse at New Baden from all over the world. Tex's wife showed me calluses on her slender fingers, the result of answering all her husband's mail.

I never met a man that seemed more sincere and modest than Tex Owens. He spoke simply and openly. Maybe, coming from anybody else, some of his little philosophies would have seemed crude. Such as his policy on how to get along in the world: "Always be yourself. Don't try to be nobody else. If you do you'll make a fool of yourself and everybody will know it but you."

The time was that Tex Owens' name rested near the top of the listener ratings in American radio, when he and his Western band playing on CBS drew up to thirty thousand pieces of fan mail a day.

The friend and I asked Tex if he'd mind getting out his guitar and singing "Cattle Call" for us. In a way I hated to ask, because I didn't think he was feeling well. But he agreed. He scooted out on the edge of the easy chair there in his living room, tuned the guitar, and talked awhile, said he really used to call cattle out on the range with that plaintive, three-quarter-time yodel in the chorus of his song.

His baritone came strong and clear, and it made you see the hungry cattle and hear the coyotes, and the cowboy was there, and the coffeepot and the campfire. It was all there.

Since that day I've not been able to get that mournful yodel out of my mind, and find myself humming it when I drive down the highway. Because the way Tex sang it, it being his own song and all, it sort of haunts you after you hear it.

I expect it was the last time Tex ever sang the old song. Two weeks later he was dead.

CHAPTER 4

"Everything should be natural."
—Teodora Saenz

Aunt Lizzie Thornton was born in the Piney Woods near Trinity. She is eighty-six years old now and the farthest she's ever been from home is Crockett, twenty-eight miles away.

Still, she gained her measure of fame. Around Trinity she is noted as an expert snuff dipper and spitter. She used to come to town every Saturday and bring along her favorite rope-bottomed chair. She'd park that chair out front of the feed store, watch the people, dip snuff with an elm twig and spit with remarkable skill. She could drown a fly at twelve feet.

Trinity folks walking on the street always gave Aunt Lizzie a wide berth when they went by the feed store. At the end of the day she'd leave behind her a solid brown snuff-juice stain, extending from her chair in a broad arc twelve to fifteen feet in diameter.

Aunt Lizzie hasn't been into town for a long time, so I got a friend to steer me out to her house to find out why. She was at home and feeling pretty well. It was a hot afternoon and she came out on her front porch, barefoot, to do her talking. She's a little thing. Likely doesn't weigh eighty-five pounds. The years have etched a thousand lines in her face and stooped her narrow shoulders, but they haven't dulled her tongue or her wits.

Now you used to hear a great deal of talk about people still hidden deep in the East Texas woods who've never been to school, never seen a train, never seen a city, never even ridden in a car. Perhaps they exist. I've not found them. Well, sure, there are a good many who've not been to school, or at least not enough to learn to read and write. And many more who can read and write like sixty who've not seen a city.

Aunt Lizzie just never did recognize any necessity for seeing a city. Once a week she went into Trinity, which has eighteen hundred people. And then she traveled twenty-eight miles that time all the way to Crockett, which is a county seat town and has more than five thousand folks and a courthouse and a county fair, and if she saw a city it'd just be the same things only more of them. So she stayed home. Except on Saturdays.

Aunt Lizzie still has her rope-bottomed chair. She pulled it out on the porch and we had a question-and-answer session.

Does she still dip snuff?

"Yessirboss," she said, using an old country expression. And saying it just that way, without any commas or spaces between the words. The "boss" part of the expression doesn't imply that she is recognizing a better. It's just a way of giving an emphatic answer.

How long has she dipped snuff now?

"I don't know. Started when I was a little girl. Ten, maybe. Used to steal snuff from my mother."

Does she think seventy-five years of snuff dipping ever hurt her?

"Naw."

Can she still spit good? Could she hit that washtub yonder by the chinaberry tree, twelve feet away?

"Could if I hadn't lost my teeth. Can't spit good without my teeth."

What would she do if the doctor told her to quit dipping?

"I'd have a dip when I wanted it. People are gonna have what they want, it don't matter what. I'm gonna have my snuff."

Why doesn't she go into town on Saturdays as she used to?

"The reason I don't," and Aunt Lizzie's eyes fired a little at the question, "I can't stand the sight of these women, wearin' pants and smokin' cigarettes. And I don't think women ought to vote, either."

Why shouldn't women vote?

"Because they're out of place at the polls. Women ought to stay in their place."

And where is that?

"At home."

How about women who work, in offices and stores?

"I don't think they ought to, but I guess it's none of my business."

Has Aunt Lizzie ever voted, even one time?

"Nosirboss."

Wouldn't she like to vote?

"Nosirboss."

Has she ever watched television?

"Saw one once. Didn't like it. That's what's makin' these children so bad, watchin' all that stuff on television."

Is Aunt Lizzie aware that men are now getting ready to fly into space and land on the moon?

"I've heard about it."

What does she think of it?

"They oughtn't to do it. That's God's moon. God put that moon there."

Does she think men will ever land on the moon?

"Naw. There's a man up there already, burnin' brush."

There's a man on the moon burning brush? How does she know that?

"Well, I can see him."

Is that what makes the moon shine, the brush burning?

"Yes."

Is that a real man up there on the moon?

"Well, I don't know. I haven't been up there to see." Aunt Lizzie thought that was a good joke and ducked her head and laughed.

But does she believe it's a real man?

"Well, it looks like a real man."

Wouldn't Aunt Lizzie like to travel? See the ocean, go to Houston, fly in an airplane?

"Nosirboss."

Does she have any particular ambition? Anything she'd especially like to do that she's never done?

"Nosirboss. I just wanta keep on doin' just what I'ma doin'."

I drove away then, and Aunt Lizzie Thornton went back to doing what she wanted to do, which was dipping snuff.

I once set out in a cloud of blissful ignorance to establish my own personal list of the ten Texas women most interesting to talk to. I gave it up because the list kept growing to twenty, and then to forty and above, and I didn't know how to chop it off. I mean how are you going to leave off a woman like Aunt Lizzie Thornton in favor of Lillie Drennan, or vice versa?

Lillie Drennan lives at Hempstead, the seat of Waller County, and is known over a wide swath of Texas as Lillie of Six-Shooter Junction. Hempstead is one of several Texas towns that enjoys remembering it was once called Six-Shooter Junction. The town earned this sobriquet in Reconstruction days when the old Houston and Texas Central Railroad was building north through Texas from Galveston, and when local papers would print such eye-catching tallies, without comment, as "Hempstead 4, Hearne 3." This wouldn't be a baseball score. It was the count on how many men were gunned down on the streets of the two towns the previous week.

Hempstead men were slow to put up their pistols. A good many years after the papers quit printing the shooting scores, a lot of hardware was still being toted around town and firing a pistol was the signal that a house or a barn or a store was afire and that everybody should fall out and help fight it. If you wanted to find out who carried a pistol and who didn't, you just stepped into the street and yelled, "Fire!" So then all the gun toters would whip out their sidearms and go to shooting at the moon, making a grand noise reminiscent of the old days when people were shooting at each other instead of just straight up.

Lillie Drennan still keeps a pistol loaded and handy. At least she had one the day I dropped by to ask her if what I heard was true—had she really quit cussing?

"Yes, that's true," Lillie said. "During Hurricane Carla in September of 1961, I had myself a hard time here. While that wind was blowing and the shingles were flying off my house, I promised God that if He'd just get me through that storm, I'd never use profane language again. And I've stuck to it, too. Oh, I might let a damn slip out now and then, but when I do I always ask God to forgive me."

That little speech tells a lot about Lillie Drennan. Cussing was once mighty natural to Lillie, almost like eating and breathing. For a quarter of a century she operated a freight line out of Hempstead. Her trucks moved a lot of crude out of Texas oil fields. She drove trucks herself and carried a pistol and practiced regularly to keep her hand in. She could tame an oil-field trucker with a stern tongue-lashing or, if that didn't work, with a swift kick in his rumble seat.

Her mellow years are upon Lillie now and she sits in her retail establishment just off the highway at Hempstead and receives visitors with grace and dignity. Long ago she gave up truck driving for a more gentle pursuit.

She runs a liquor store.

There's a lot about Lillie that seems average. Her features are just good American woman features. Her voice is husky, but not extraordinarily. Her hair is gray, just as the hair of most women past sixty-five is gray.

But her eyes. Now there is where Lillie shows through. You'll not find snappier, darker, younger eyes in the face of a girl of eighteen. When Lillie speaks of Hempstead's Six-Shooter Junction days or recalls some tale of her years in the driver's seat of a tandem rig, those eyes kindle Lillie's old fire. Then they grow cool and sad when she speaks of lost things. Like Miss Snooks.

Miss Snooks was a dog, and Lillie's friend, companion, and protector for years. "She was a hearing-ear dog," Lillie told me. "Some people can't see, they have seeing-eye dogs. I've had trouble with my hearing for years, and Snooks was my ears. Nobody could slip up on me while she was around. She was with me thirteen years and four months."

When Miss Snooks died, Lillie was obliged to install in her house an intricate burglar alarm to protect herself and her merchandise.

"I've got amplifiers stuck all over this place," she told me. "See those wires? If you just rap on the outside wall, the alarm goes off. If you walk on my roof, that'll set it off. If you just touch the front door when I'm closed, even that'll set 'er to going. Then I've still got my pistol. I don't go out and practice any more like I once did, but I could hit a man with it if he was standing up here in front of me."

[69]

Lillie's friends around Hempstead say she doesn't seem like the same person since she quit cussing. But she sticks to the vow she made to the Lord during the hurricane and puts in dangs where the damns used to be, and hecks where the hells were. In situations where dang and heck just don't seem appropriate, she uses the initials for stronger terms, and in this way manages to get by.

In Freeport there's a little section of town called the Barrio, where the homes of Latin-American people are concentrated. In Texas, Latin Americans are most often referred to in daily conversation as Mexicans. Of course they're not Mexicans. A man born in San Antonio and named Jose Garcia is not a Mexican any more than you are an Englishman if you were born in Dallas and had a grandfather named Hastings.

But the ancestors of most Texas Latins were Mexicans and in some towns these Spanish-speaking people tend to stick together, live apart from the mass of Anglos, and preserve at least part of their Mexican heritage. In Freeport's Barrio, for example, you find some homes in which little if any English is spoken, and at times you can go into a neighborhood like the one where Teodora Saenz lives and get the feeling you are down in some state of Mexico—Nuevo León or Tamaulipas.

Teodora Saenz once told me her father was Spanish and her mother was Polish. And so it is that she has a Latin name, blue eyes, and red hair.

Well, her hair was red at one time. She is a great-grandmother now and Dora's hair is a beautiful silver and stands high on her head in braided splendor, making a mighty attractive crown for her round little face.

Within the Barrio, Dora occupies a somewhat peculiar position. Her duties touch upon those of a doctor, welfare worker, truant officer, mother confessor, and likely a number of others I haven't heard about. To illustrate, imagine that a young boy happened to pass Dora's house on a school day, going in a direction that wouldn't take him to the schoolhouse. She would be apt to pounce on him and give him an unshirted piece of her mind about the value of an education and send him scooting back toward school. But if that same schoolboy, now, got into trouble or needed help of any kind, he would come running to Miss Dora and he would get the help he needed.

A lot of the natives of the Barrio have left and gone out and made their mark in the world, and dozens of these yet write to Dora as to their own mothers. Back during the war years, when young men everywhere found it necessary to prove the particulars of their births as they entered military service, scores of Barrio men flocked to Dora Saenz to get affidavits. For she is a midwife, and served as chief administrator for many blessed events there in the Barrio. But she is retired from that practice now, and seems hesitant to discuss the details.

In her spotless and orderly house Dora raised first her own children, then "somebody else's," then her grandchildren, and now her great-grandchildren visit her there. "I've been both man and woman around my house," she says, "since 1928."

That was the year her second husband, Santiago Saenz, was killed in Duval County, where he served the law as a pistolero. It's said that after the death of her husband Dora refused many marriage offers. And you believe it, too, for it is not hard to imagine that Dora's red hair, blue eyes, and saucy manner made her an attractive widow in 1928.

If she chose, Dora could tell stories that would make fascinating reading. About the joys and sorrows and the drama of the life that goes on in the Barrio. But she doesn't, and her friends say the reason is that she is somehow involved in all of them, most often as a great benefactress, and so doesn't consider it appropriate to speak of such things.

One day she was talking to me about her career as a midwife, though, and the conversation touched upon the antiseptic surroundings into which most of today's babies are born. Dora deplores that. Doesn't think it's right.

"Everything," she said, "should be natural."

What she meant, specifically, is that she wouldn't give you a plugged peso for all your germ-free obstetrical wards in hospitals. And she bristles at the mention of drugs administered to women in labor. Doesn't think such drugs do anything but harm.

I've remembered Dora's "everything should be natural" because the statement seems to sum up her views on everything, not just childbirth. There are weaker philosophies. You and I and the family doctor are at liberty to differ with Dora's notion of what childbirth ought to be like. But there is this to consider—during her career of midwifery, Dora never lost a mother or a baby.

My notion is that the day Miss Annie Spinn died was a sad one for the little city of Brenham. The town lost a heavy touch of color with Miss Annie's passing.

On one of my earliest visits to Brenham I saw Miss Annie pull up in front of a drugstore and double-park. Double-parking on the courthouse square is normally frowned on by Brenham police, but they permitted Miss Annie to park where she pleased. Anyway she could hardly park head-in, because she drove a sorrel mare hitched to a buggy. This wasn't in 1915, now. Miss Annie was still driving that mare in the early 1960s. She had been coming to town in the buggy so many years that gray-haired people around town couldn't remember when she hadn't.

[72]

There in front of the drugstore Miss Annie collared the first passer-by and issued orders for him to go in and send out a clerk. Miss Annie expected curb service and she got it. She also got the right-of-way on all streets no matter which way she headed or turned, and there was an unwritten traffic law in Brenham that everybody was supposed to watch out for Miss Annie Spinn. She was apt to execute a U-turn at just any intersection, even right there on the court-house square, and you had to look sharp to miss her.

In her late years Miss Annie's eyesight wasn't much good, and the sorrel mare's wasn't either. I always thought it spoke well of the people of Brenham, the way they watched out for Miss Annie and her mare.

I stopped a traffic officer and asked him if it ever occurred to the police department to give Miss Annie a ticket for her violations. He said no.

Then I eased over to the corner where the drugstore clerk had answered Miss Annie's summons. She wanted a bulb for her flashlight. The clerk went back in and brought out a bulb. It wasn't the right size so he went back in and brought out another. Miss Annie looked that one over, thought about it awhile, and decided not to buy the bulb. Just didn't like it. So she spoke to the mare, which wheeled around and pulled the buggy through a U-turn and trotted off through the downtown traffic on the wrong side of the street.

A few months after that I went to Brenham hoping to talk to Miss Annie, and got directed out north of town, where she was seen headed a few minutes earlier. I caught the buggy just as the mare was pulling it off the pavement onto the dirt road that leads to Miss Annie's old home three miles outside town.

I'm pretty sure Miss Annie was asleep when I drove up beside the buggy. They say she often took naps while riding,

[73]

but it didn't really matter because the mare knew where Miss Annie was going and anyway could see better than her mistress and didn't need any steering.

Miss Annie's brown little weathered face lighted up considerably when I finally got her stopped and asked a question or two. A three-gallon cream can was at her feet. For goodness knows how many years Miss Annie came into town to sell butter, and in later years she just brought cream to the creamery. I asked her that day if she ever had any trouble with the traffic in town.

"No-o-o-o," she said, "not a bit."

But didn't anybody ever complain about the buggy and the mare being on the streets?

"Well, there was one fellow that complained one time, and when I heard it I went straight to the chief of police and asked him if it was all right if I kept coming to town. And he said I could come to town in this buggy just whenever I pleased. I've been paying taxes in Washington County longer than anybody that's complaining about my buggy. I've got to go now. I'm pretty busy. It's been mighty dry out on my place and I've had to haul water from town every day." She spoke to the mare and the buggy moved off, leaving me standing there in the road with a lot more questions to ask.

Miss Annie lived alone on that farm until she was well up into her eighties, and then she had to go to a rest home, where she died. Shortly before she had to leave home I was passing through Brenham and there was Miss Annie double-parked in front of the post office, waiting for somebody to bring out her mail. She got curb service at the post office just the same as she did at the drugstore. The town has not been nearly so interesting since she's gone.

People still like to tell about the time Miss Annie met and conquered the U. S. Army. One of these big military

[74]

convoys was rolling through town. If you've ever sat at an intersection and waited for one of those things to pass, you know that they don't give the right-of-way to anybody.

But Miss Annie knew nothing of that and wouldn't have cared if she did. She trotted the mare right out in the path of the convoy, which screeched to a halt to keep from ramming the buggy. I'm sorry I missed the sight of that string of GI trucks parked there waiting for Miss Annie's buggy and sorrel mare to pass.

Texas women worth knowing are found in some almighty unexpected places. About three o'clock one terrifically hot July day I was cruising around the little city of Luling, some fifty miles east of San Antonio, and a sign on a white residence stopped me. You'll see thousands of similarly built houses in little Texas towns. Frame construction, white paint that needs a fresh coat, a porch running all the way across the front, and a couple of hackberry trees that do their best to shade the yard.

The sign said the residence housed the A. C. Bridges Library. I stopped and knocked and a woman's voice, clear and loaded with authority, commanded me to enter. I walked in and even before I could see its owner the voice asked, "Do you have change for fifty cents?"

The voice belonged to Louise B. Witt. Behind a low table in one of the front rooms she sat and waited on a couple of library patrons come to rent books. Mrs. Witt took the change from me and said in that same commanding tone, "If you're interested in books, go ahead and look around. If not just sit down there and wait." I took the chair and watched Mrs. Witt wait on the book renters. She was wearing a pale lavender print dress, long-sleeved and held high and tight at her throat by a pearl brooch. Behind the spectacles her face showed that peculiar combination of sternness and gentleness I have seen on the faces of schoolteachers who have taught a long, long time and who love children but try to pretend they don't. Her gray hair swept back a little. It seemed to be held in place by a tight hair net, but it wasn't. There was still a problem making change. Mrs. Witt owed one of the book renters a penny.

"It's all right," the patron said. "Just forget it."

"No, no," Mrs. Witt said, "we won't forget it." She took the customer's name and address and made a record of the debt in the big ledger before her.

That room was almost unbearably hot. There were no blinds on the windows and the midafternoon July sun bore through the glass and glared off the books—some shelved and catalogued, many others just stacked about on tables.

"I can't use air-conditioning," Mrs. Witt was saying. The customers had left. "Can't even sit in front of a fan. Gives me neuralgia."

She began talking about the library. Said it had 2500 volumes and they all belong to her and she rents the books and doesn't make any money at it. And the reason she does this, her mother (the late Anne C. Bridges) always wanted Luling to have a library. She's been on the job ever since she retired from schoolteaching in 1955.

"I taught school forty-four years." As she talked, Mrs. Witt looked critically over a half-worked jigsaw puzzle spread on the low table. "I taught twenty-three years in public school and twenty-one years in private kindergarten. I quit the public schools just before the state installed the teacher retirement program. When I started this library, a friend gave me a hundred dollars to help buy books, and I've still got some of that money in the bank."

I looked around and chose a book and asked how much it rented for.

"Give me a quarter and you can keep it a month. You

know, the only book I ever had that paid for itself was *Grapes of Wrath*. I really cleaned up on that one."

She turned the big ledger around so I could see it. "Look here. Last month, June, I had the best month I've ever had."

The ledger showed that total receipts from book rentals in June were $5.95.

"No, wait now," Mrs. Witt said, turning the ledger back around. "Martha Jane paid me fifty cents that I didn't enter." She made the entry. "There, that puts me over six dollars for June." She seemed pleased.

That room was mighty warm. When I left my shirt was soaked with sweat. Outside, the hackberry leaves hung limp in the July sun and the heat waves danced off the street. I got in the car, turned the air-conditioner up to the top peg, and drove down the highway thinking what a good thing it is not to have neuralgia.

The first time I saw Mary Baca she was slipping out the side door of her little café in El Campo with a paper sack full of kolaches, those delicious little Czech pastries. The café at the time was full of cash customers. But what she had noticed, having a sharp eye for such details, was that a couple of hungry youngsters were standing outside because they didn't have the money to come in. She gave the kolaches to the boys and, like as not, inspected them to see if their ears needed scrubbing. And if they did, I know she scrubbed them.

Mary won't remember that, because she's done it so many times the details escape her. Around El Campo, she is a sort of a one-woman public welfare department. She likes to help people and has just a lot of fun doing it.

She is a plump little woman with a great store of energy and a strange radiant quality in her plain features. When she was two years old she came to Texas with her family

[77]

from Czechoslovakia and did her growing up on a Wharton County farm not far from El Campo. As a girl she would stomp down the row in a cotton patch, chopping Johnson grass with a gooseneck hoe and telling herself that one day she would learn to speak English, become a U.S. citizen, and "get to be president of something."

Mary married a farmer named Ed Hlavaty, who was soon to become an invalid. To make a living, Mary would put her two babies in an old Model T Ford and drive over the countryside, selling notions and lotions and cosmetics to Czech farmers' wives. She also ran the farm. And at night she went to school to learn the five hundred words of English necessary to get her U.S. citizenship papers. While thus burdened, one day on her rounds she found a handicapped child that nobody wanted. She immediately loved that child, so she took him home and nursed him and kept him for twelve years.

Debts kept piling up for the Hlavatys, so they sold the farm to pay off their creditors. When the books were cleared, they had exactly fifty dollars left. They moved into town, to El Campo, and Mary went to a lumberyard with a question—what kind of a store building could be built for fifty dollars?

The "store" measured eight by ten feet. It stood across the street from one of El Campo's elementary schools. There Mary sold homemade candy and nickel hamburgers to the students. At night she would pick up her entire store stock, throw it in the Model T, and drive over to a produce company where a crew of men worked all night processing turkeys. Until 1 or 2 a.m. she'd sell hamburgers to the produce workers, then fold up and go back to the store and be ready to open up to serve the students the next morning. And she got part-time work at *Svobada,* a Czech-language newspaper in El Campo, where she gathered news items and sold ads.

Ed Hlavaty then succumbed to his long illness, and after that Mary bought a small grocery store. Two years later she married Fred Baca.

Things were a little better now. Mary had always dreamed of owning and operating a beauty shop. Her husband Fred argued that it wouldn't pay. Mary opened the shop anyway, and despite her tireless efforts at making the shop a paying proposition, it lost money steadily. She couldn't bear to admit defeat. She would slip money out of the grocery-store cashbox to pay the beauty shop's expenses so her husband Fred wouldn't know the shop was losing money. This may not have been sound economics but it was characteristic of Mary Baca, who believes a person ought to finish what he starts.

Now Mary had four children of her own, plus the youngster she had taken in. Then she found a hungry twelve-year-old girl, brought her home, gave her a good scrubbing, and set her a place at the table. The girl lived with the Bacas for three years.

Finally doctors told Mary she'd have to slow down. She was working in the store, caring for six children at home, running all over the county to take sacks of groceries to hungry families. Or to deliver a mattress to somebody she'd learned didn't have one. Or to give clothes to those who were ragged. She developed an uncanny skill for searching out people that needed help, learned the knack of helping them and making it seem they weren't really taking charity at all. She also fulfilled her cotton-patch vow when a local Czech church lodge elected her its chief officer. She had become "president of something" at last.

But on doctor's orders Fred and Mary Baca sold their grocery store. They moved to California, stayed two weeks, didn't like it, came back home, and began building the small café that Mary still operates.

Visiting in a home for aged people in the neighboring city of Wharton one day, Mary met an old and sick Czech woman who doctors said might live two weeks. On sight, Mary loved this old woman that nobody else loved. She put her in the car and brought her home, to make her last days comfortable. The woman lived twelve years, most of those in a new air-conditioned trailer house that Mary and Fred Baca bought and parked out behind their home.

This gave Mary an idea. Why couldn't she build a home for elderly Czech people? The coastal area of Texas abounds in Czech-descended citizens, hardy folk who often live to advanced ages.

The job took years, but now the Czech Catholic Home for the Aged stands at Hillje, a little community in central Wharton County, and many of Mary's beloved "old folks" live there in comfort. Hundreds of people—at Mary Baca's behest, of course—donated money toward the construction of the home and worked long and hard to get it built. But nobody will deny that the home is there because of Mary Baca, and some will say it was as if Mary built it with her own hands.

During the fund-raising campaign, Mary had to move in more sophisticated circles than she was accustomed to. She was terrified, and highly self-conscious of her broken English. She was always apologizing for it. Then one day a polished gentleman she met sat her down and lectured her long and sternly about her accent. He said some of the smartest and best citizens of this nation speak with foreign accents, and he didn't want her ever again to be apologizing for the way she spoke. Since that day Mary has never hesitated to speak out, and the accent be hanged.

Once the home for the aged was built and operating,

[80]

Mary had no more work to do than three average people, so she sat down and wrote a book. A cook book, containing a hundred fifty Czech recipes and dozens of "compliments of" advertisements. All the money from the sale of the book went toward paying off the mortgage on the home at Hillje. Mary even wrote to the President—Dwight Eisenhower was in the White House then—and got a reply from him and a photograph of himself and Mamie that went in the cook book. This was a miraculous development to Mary, to think that the immigrant Czech girl who once chopped cotton and dreamed of speaking English would be corresponding with the president of the United States.

About once a year I drop by the little café in El Campo and listen to Mary talk awhile. I go for selfish reasons. On days when the world seems a dreary, spiritless place, I can sit and listen to Mary and get my enthusiasm recharged. If you were to go see her—and have no doubt she would be happy to have you—you would understand. She has an almost childish enthusiasm about everything on earth that's good. As for what's bad, why, she is enthusiastic about that, too, because all it represents is an opportunity to go to work and get it corrected. This super-enthusiasm might seem insincere and begin to pall if it were displayed by anybody else I know. On Mary it fits like a silk glove.

I stopped at Mary's place one afternoon just after she'd returned from a visit to California to see relatives. She was taken around to many of the tourist attractions in California and was enthralled by them all, but as close as I could make out she was most enthusiastic about finding eggs selling for thirty-five cents a dozen at Lake Arrowhead. Listen to her talk awhile.

"I was just amazed," she said, stirring a big pot of figs bubbling on her kitchen stove and setting out a tray of coffee and kolaches. "Think of it—thirty-five cents a dozen and way up there in the mountains. And salmon for sixty-seven cents, which is the same I pay for it right here at home. Listen, did you ever see the cavern at Sonora? We saw it on our way home. Beautiful, beautiful. I've been to the cave in New Mexico—Carlsbad—but Sonora is more beautiful. Not so big as Carlsbad, but the colors, beautiful, and right here in Texas. Tell all your friends about it. I brought home some circulars and you can take some and leave them around. Remind me I want to give you some dates I brought from California when you leave."

You ought to know that these quotes don't really show how Mary talks. Her Czech accent, which adds so much to what she says, just can't be reproduced on paper.

A small elderly woman in a neat print dress shuffled through Mary's living room during my visit. "That's one of my little grandmothers," Mary said. Not her real grand-mother, you understand. Just another person Mary has taken in. "She didn't have anybody, and she wanted to stay with me. There wasn't any room at the old folks' home, so she is here now. I've got two others with me now. I enjoy them so much. We don't smoke at our house, and we don't drink, and we save our little money and we take the trip in summer. It doesn't cost us much because we have so many kinfolks everywhere. Why, I brought back $132 from California. Here, try one other of the kolaches. Is there a cabbage kolache here? I don't think so. I made cabbage kolaches in California and these rich people were there, very nice people, and I'm so proud I met them, and one man said he didn't like kolaches. But he kept eating and I noticed him slip one in his pocket to take home. It doesn't sound good to put cabbage in a kolache but it's good, and the recipe is in our cook book that you have. Oh, listen, the next trip I make, I want to go back to Europe. So many of my friends go and I've never been. I want to go back to the little town in Czechoslovakia where I was born. I was two years old when I left but I think when I am there I will know where everything is because I have all the pictures from there. And right near my home town, only several miles, is a place where the Blessed Mother appeared just a few years ago and I want to see that. It's a place where a spring is, the same as at Lourdes. Nothing much has been said about it because the communists are against anything religious. Some people have drunk the water from the spring and it has powers. A nun that I know who lives near here was in a terrible car wreck and doctors said she would not ever walk again. She had relatives in Czechoslovakia and some of the water from the spring they sent to her. Just not long ago I looked out and here was the sister driving up and getting out of the car. I was amazed. Remind me to give you a jar of my hot relish when you go, and don't forget to tell your friends about the cavern at Sonora."

Well, that's just a sample.

In addition to keeping three "grandmothers" there in her home, Mary is now operating an unofficial old-clothes charity agency. Her husband Fred built her a long rack in the attic, and she has a stock of clothing up there that would do justice to a secondhand store. Mary somehow knows the sizes of people in her orbit of operation who need clothing, and she hands it out according to their needs. "I'm having such a good time with my old clothes," she says, in a tone you or I might use if we talked about how we enjoyed playing a fashionable card game or driving a new car.

One day Mary told me she almost got put in jail. I must have sat upright at this astonishing news. She explained she got involved in an argument with the representatives of a welfare agency about a certain charity case. Mary can get her dander up when she thinks one of her needy friends is being mistreated.

Well, of course the idea of Mary Baca being in jail is just preposterous. There isn't a jail standing that would hold her. The walls of the thing would fall in with shame.

CHAPTER 5

*"I've lost only two elections in my life, and one of
them was on purpose."*

—Goree King

"We'll take it sort of easy," George Shelfer said, shifting
gears. "I just put new bearings in 'er three days ago, and
she's still a little stiff."

The old red and white bus pulled out of Brenham on
time—11:30 A.M. Its destination was Bryan, forty-five miles
up the Brazos River. In fact Bryan is the only destination
the bus ever has, except when it turns around and heads
back to Brenham.

A tag over the driver's seat announced we were riding
in Vehicle Number 1 of Shelfer Buslines. It is the only
vehicle Shelfer Buslines has. George Shelfer is Shelfer Buslines' chief executive, chief driver, chief mechanic, chief
porter, chief everything.

Our cargo included five sacks of chicken feed, a box of
beef for Charlie Schulte's General Store at Clay Station,
four paying passengers, a fifth passenger riding on credit,
and a sixth who was just deadheading, to see how a one-
man, one-vehicle bus line operates.

For more than seventeen years, seven days a week,
George Shelfer has driven his red and white bus two round
trips between Bryan and Brenham. A killing schedule, so
Shelfer takes it easy even when the bearings in the bus
aren't new.

[85]

Shelfer is a small, wiry individual that likely wouldn't gain a pound if he took on twenty thousand calories a day. He's old enough that he spent twenty-five years in the car repair business before he became a one-man bus line in 1947.

"Pretty soon," Shelfer said, steering the old bus off the state highway onto a farm road that runs up the Brazos Bottom, "I'll jerk the head off and grind those valves." He leaned forward and cocked his head a little, as a natural mechanic does when he listens for trouble symptoms in an engine.

When he makes a major repair job like that, it's a night chore. The two round trips completed for the day, he enlists help from his son Harold, who's in the garage business at Snook. Snook is one of the scheduled stops on the run, though the bus makes a lot more unscheduled stops than scheduled. Shelfer and his son tear down the engine, repair it, and put it back together in one night, so the bus will be ready to roll again the next morning.

A repair Shelfer doesn't bother to make is on his speedometer, which wore out in 1956. Not that it matters much, since Shelfer knows how fast he is going from the sound of his engine. As for his total mileage, he doesn't seem interested in that. But by my arithmetic, when a man drives 1260 miles a week and 65,520 miles a year, in seventeen years he has put in better than a million miles. In the same vehicle, over the same route.

Rolling toward Clay Station at thirty mph, Shelfer showed me his blue certificate of operation, issued by the State Railroad Commission, the agency that regulates public transportation in Texas. The certificate states that Shelfer Buslines' service is a "convenience and a necessity."

The Railroad Commission is right. Without Shelfer and his red bus, scores of residents living along the banks of

[86]

the Brazos in Washington and Burleson counties would have no way to get to town for groceries.

When you ride Shelfer's bus you learn to be patient. At Clay Station we stopped and Shelfer disappeared into Charlie Schulte's store and stayed maybe twenty minutes. He finally came out munching on some soda crackers and rattrap cheese. Shelfer brings meat to Schulte as a favor, and when Shelfer has a breakdown out on the road somewhere, Schulte goes out and helps him with repairs.

We chugged off and stopped again not an eighth of a mile later and Shelfer went in the Little Daisy Cafe. Somebody at the café had car trouble and had asked Shelfer to take a look. He came out and raised the hood on the car and poked around for a good while. Two or three café customers watched critically, mumbling suggestions occasionally. The passengers in Shelfer's bus sat patiently and talked of the weather and about who was sick and about what the farmers in the river bottom were paying for cotton chopping. Not a one showed any sign of irritation at the delay.

Later on I saw why. It was because every one of them, before they left the bus, had some special service to ask of Shelfer. One, for example, requested a stop at the Clay Station Post Office so he could get his mail.

At Becker's Store we stopped to let another passenger go in and pick up a package he had left there earlier that morning. The passenger stayed a good while and Shelfer sat slumped at the wheel and waited as patiently as the passenger waited for him at the café.

On up the river bottom north of Clay Station, an elderly gent carrying a flour sack got off the bus and trudged off down the turnrow of a cotton field. "That's Mr. Booth," Shelfer said, shifting gears slowly as we pulled out again. "Don't know his first name. But he's a fine man. He rides into Brenham with me pretty often with his sack to buy something. If the price isn't right, sometimes he'll come back home with an empty sack. Or maybe he'll get back on in Brenham and ride to Bryan with me to get a better deal."

I looked back at Mr. Booth. He moved slowly along the turnrow with the flour sack thrown across his shoulder. I supposed prices in town didn't suit him that day, because the sack was empty.

Just south of Snook we stopped and Shelfer helped Leroy Hoskins carry the five sacks of chicken feed off the bus and up to the house.

Shelfer considers such services well within his responsibilities as a bus line operator. He takes seriously those words "convenience and a necessity" on the state certificate of operation. Sometimes he'll show up at the bus station in Brenham with a small bottle—a prescription that some sick person out on the line needs refilled. If he has time he'll walk up to the drugstore and get the medicine. If not, Emma Hauck goes out for it. She operates the bus station, and a café in conjunction. Her homemade bread, which she bakes fresh every morning there in the café, makes that bus station a regular stop for a great many people who never ride Shelfer's bus. Emma is a truly fine cook who loves to watch people eat. One day a college boy sat there in the café waiting for the bus and consumed three-fourths of one of Emma's fresh-baked two-pound loaves of bread, "without butter or water or anything with it." And it pleased Emma greatly when Shelfer reported the next day that the young man had finished the other fourth of the loaf before the bus crossed the Brazos.

At Snook, Shelfer turned a corner and a man at a garage looked up and waved him on. A sign that there were no passengers to be picked up. "That's Pint Rubach," Shelfer told me. "Sometimes I'll pick up a car part for him in Brenham or Bryan, and sometimes he'll clean a set of plugs for me."

No money ever changes hands in these transactions. It's all a matter of swapping favors, and not keeping count.

At Lawrence Grocery, another stop to let a passenger go in and cash a check. Quarter of a mile later still another, for Shelfer to carry on a brief visit with his son Harold.

Turning east to head across the Brazos River, a young Negro boy flagged Shelfer down. He got on the bus and held a lengthy conversation before he sat down, without paying a fare, and then Shelfer drove on. The boy hadn't any money and had made a deal to ride on credit. "I let a good many of 'em ride on promise," Shelfer said. "I don't lose any fares that way much. Only just once in a while. I figure if they beat me out of half a dollar, then it's worth that to find out they won't pay."

We got into Bryan at one-forty. Distance traveled—forty-five miles. Traveling time—two hours and ten minutes. Which I thought was not bad, considering the stops for conveniences and necessities.

Since the day I rode with him, I've passed George Shelfer in his red bus many, many times and have kept up a waving acquaintance with him. Now and then I see him stopped on the road, waiting for Charlie Schulte or Pint Rubach to come help him with repairs. One morning I drove up behind his bus, stalled, on a steep hill just east of Brenham. I slowed down to ask if he needed help, but the help he needed was just behind me. It was a cattle truck, the driver of which eased his rig gently into the rear of Shelfer's bus, nudged it over the hilltop and pushed till it got going again.

A few miles below the bridge that George Shelfer drives his rambling red bus across four times daily, the Navasota River contributes its contents to the Brazos.

Follow the Navasota upstream about two counties and you come to Goree King's house. It stands on a hill on the Leon County side of the river. From that rock house King carries on a variety of activities, such as raising cows and settling arguments.

On first meeting King sets up as a colorful and polite and yet a mysterious fellow. His manner seemed to me to say, "I'll be glad to have you sit here awhile and visit, but don't push me too far or get to nosing into my business."

Perhaps the mystery around King springs from the fact that, while his appearance fails to suggest it, he is a man of great influence in his little part of Texas. He is small, and almighty thin, with high cheekbones and the leanest of jaws. He might be the last person you'd pick out of a crowd as a citizen with personal magnetism, yet he is certainly that.

As a way of explaining, let us say that a young fellow along the Navasota River in Leon or Robertson County finds himself in difficulty. A difficulty, say, with the law. The first advice he is apt to get from his elders is, "The best thing you can do is see Goree King. He'll go and talk to the right people and straighten everything out."

King's reputation for being able to "straighten everything out" is such that a lot of Texas lawyers who know him often say, when trying to untangle an impossible legal situation, "It'd take Goree King to set this one straight."

King claims he has no idea how he got started serving as a riverbank attorney, or a lawyer without portfolio, as some of his friends call him. But he is thoroughly established in that position. Neighbors come to his rock house to have disagreements settled. Friends stop by to ask if he will intercede with a prosecuting attorney. Or to have a talk with a judge that's about to hear a case.

An attorney introducing a Texas district judge to Goree

King said, "Judge, this is Lawyer King. He lives on the east side of Robertson County and the west side of Leon County, and if he ever comes into your court wanting anything you may as well give it to him, because he's going to get it anyway."

The key to King's ability to straighten out knotty problems may lie in the way he has of leaning forward in his seat, propping one elbow on his knee, and saying just one thing after another that makes sense.

He has prevented many a fight in this way. It is said also that he is equally effective in stopping fights after they have started, though King does not speak of that. Nor do his many friends in the little community of Marquez, east of the Navasota a few miles, where King buys his groceries. There are many things in the background of Marquez that aren't spoken of, at least not to guys carrying pencils and notebooks. Marquez has a bootleggin', whiskey-cookin', fist-fightin' history.

It wasn't until I had left King's house, after the first and only time I saw him, that it occurred to me I'd not really learned a thing about the man. All I'd written down during the visit were some of his expressions. They came thick and fast and new and fresh and I got to watching for them so closely they threw me off the track. While King is sitting there with his elbow on his knee and delivering his wisdoms, it is impossible to dislike him. There's that beautiful way he has of saying things, with calm, earthy understatement.

See if we can catch some of it. When he describes a situation that has made King and his friends fighting mad, he simply smiles and says, "That didn't suit hardly any of us."

When he describes a drunk man: "He had the whiskey some."

The dress of a city slicker: "A preacher-coated man, with buttons in the back."

Two enemies who were so at odds that even King failed to settle their differences: "They never did get in a good humor."

What a fine thing it would be if Goree King were really a practicing attorney instead of a river-bottom cowman. He would pack 'em Perry Mason deep in the courtrooms with those phrases. And how he could have bent the ear of a jury.

But King's true love is not lawyering. It's politics. He labors long and hard in local elections. And some that aren't so local. A politician who runs for an office in Goree King's circle of operation is making a fatal error if he fails to weigh in the potency of the riverbank lawyer's influence.

His record of working on the winning side in elections is enough to demoralize a candidate who finds himself lined up against King's camp. "I've lost only two elections in my life," King says, "and one of them was on purpose."

The only question I asked Goree King concerned the methods he uses to influence voters. I got a polite answer that really said he didn't care to discuss it. But I have my notion that King's methods of handling voters would make a thick chapter in a book about how rural politics work in Texas.

But he dismisses his successful politicking, as well as his ability to settle arguments, with this simple appraisal:

"Well, I don't dislike anybody. And I can work on both sides, and first thing you know, everything's fixed real pretty."

Then there's Mangy Springer.

Mangy and Goree King live not thirty-five miles apart.

Whether the two ever met I don't know, but if they did I'm sorry I wasn't there to hear the conversation.

To a person given to pasting labels on people, Mangy might be classed as an anachronism. I wouldn't call him that, certainly not to his face, because I'd be afraid he'd slug me. But it's a fact that Alvin Thomas Springer, which is Mangy's square handle, is living in the wrong age. He should have been a cowboy in the trail-driving days.

As it is, he is a cowboy anyway, on the Lazy A Ranch in Robertson County near Hearne. He's in his late twenties now. About five feet eleven, a hundred sixty pounds, blue-green eyes, sandy hair, and a light way of walking about, as if he might be tough in a fist fight. Living in the century previous to this one, as he should have, Mangy would have looked just right with a gun in a slick holster strapped low on his thigh.

The thing a person must admire Mangy for is that he is clearly the real article, here in a state where so many of the cowboy-booted set are now the soda-fountain type. I mean he's not just a hand that can saddle a horse and follow a bunch of fat Herefords from one pasture to another. He can get up on a green horse and break him. He busts broncs as a sideline to his cowboying.

"I was raised in Mississippi," Mangy told me one day when I caught him in a talkative mood on the Lazy A. "Left there when about seventeen. Now I've been around stock and done ranch and farm work all my life, and I seen I had to get something else to do. Well, I taken ahold of first one thing and then another. Drove a bulldozer four, five years. Still drive one here on the ranch sometimes.

"This horse breakin', it's mostly just a sideline with me. No, I never do any rodeoin'. I don't mind puttin' a saddle on an old horse and breakin' him out, but I don't see no

[93]

sense in a man goin' off rodeoin' and gettin' hurt and laid up. I got responsibilities. I got a wife and two kids."

Mangy spoke a bit about horse breaking, and I include the little speech mainly because I love to hear him talk.

"Horse oughta be a three-year-old, two and a half at the least, when you break him out. All you do, you just get a bridle on him, and a light saddle, and you get up there and get you a good seat, and try to hold his old head up. If you can't, well, you just turn 'im loose and let 'im buck till he bucks out.

"You get bucked off, there ain't but just one thing to do, and that's get back up there and take your seat again. One might buck ten, fifteen minutes the first day, and buck some every time you get on 'im for a week. Some mightn't not buck any at all.

"Well, sure, I get bucked off. Had one here the other day. A mare six years old. She'd been broke before and turned out to pasture three or four years. That's the worst kind. Kind that'll kill you. I come off her and plowed me up some ground.

"Now you take a good blooded horse that's not broke, may be worth a hundred dollars. Same horse broke and cleaned up'll bring two hundred dollars, maybe two fifty. I charge thirty dollars to break a horse. Don't make no difference whether he bucks or he don't. It's all thirty dollars. And I don't care what kind of an old outlaw it is, either. We'll try 'im. We'll get on 'im."

The "we" included Dan Dodd, Lazy A foreman who participates in the horse breaking with Mangy sometimes.

People around Robertson County who know Mangy carry a great respect for him, which Mangy earned as the result of his ability to be just as tough, or as polite, or as courteous, or as rough, or as congenial as the situation in which he finds himself dictates.

[94]

A somewhat scholarly friend of Mangy's once told me, "There's something grand in the gentlemanly manner Mangy displays when he holds a horse for a lady, and hands her up in the saddle. Perhaps what makes me notice it is I know that not ten minutes earlier Mangy was engaged in some violent pursuit, like riding a bronc or loading an outlaw steer."

It's true there is much violence in the life of a man like Mangy. Not wild and destructive violence, but action, physical performance. He takes a pride in accomplishment involving danger and challenge.

"We got a sayin' around here on the place," Mangy told me. "We say there ain't nothin' we can't do. Like we pen a lot of wild cattle for people. We'll pen anybody's wild cattle. We penned some at Humble that was down in that brush and hadn't seen a man in seven, eight years. Didn't even know what a man was. Dan bought a hundred head of 'em and they told us, they said, 'You'll never load them cows. You'll kill ever one of 'em.' Well, we loaded 'em. And we did kill a few, too."

What Mangy admires most in his associates is physical toughness and agility and just plain guts. He made a brief statement to me that remains a high favorite among all the sentences I ever wrote down. He was speaking of the toughness of many of the men with whom he is associated in breaking horses and penning wild cattle. Men older than he is; men he can look up to and respect. I think the statement reveals much of Mangy's view of this life and the things of value he finds in it. He said:

"Some of these old coots around here is still pretty rank."

It isn't likely Mangy could come up with anything to say that would better express his admiration for his friends, for to be rank is to be a man, and that's the most important thing.

But just as worthy as the thought expressed in the statement is the fact that it stands as a pure and unvarnished example of the Texas language in its basic form. A sentence like that has, to me, the beauty, the rhythm of poetry. It is the language of the people who built my state, and I take a pride in it.

And I am pained a little at the recollection of the brief years when I was ashamed of it. Those were the World War II years, which seem so long ago, when men from all over this nation were thrown together to communicate. I didn't take kindly to the kidding that all Texans got about their accents, and I even tried to change. I didn't manage to, and I'm glad now.

Mangy Springer would snort at this, but I find a vague comfort, difficult to explain, in knowing that men of his cut are still among us. Men who live by their wits and their muscles and their fortitude, and who believe them that works eats and them that doesn't don't, and who are, praise them, still too rank and independent to run looking for a federal subsidy every time a hunger pain hits them in the belly.

Back down the Brazos Valley from Mangy Springer's stomping ground, you can find Pop Brymer sitting in a rocking chair in a red frame house on West Mustang Street in Caldwell.

"I only just wish," he said to me from the rocking chair one day, "that I'd stayed in the army."

Pop is a Spanish-American War veteran. Close to ninety years old. Looking at him and noting his military appearance, I imagined he was a distinguished soldier seventy years ago. Just for a moment I pictured him as a spit-and-polish lieutenant, leading a company of infantry and storming through the barbed-wire entanglements at Morro Castle in 1898.

Pop snickered at the idea. "No, I was Number Two in the rear rank and that's the way I liked it. All I ever did was follow the guy in front of me."

Which is one of the most refreshing things I ever heard an old soldier say in appraising his military career. Somehow most all old soldiers you meet were at least captains and won a war somewhere with their brains if not their courage and of course they end up being bores.

"I went to Cuba after the war was over," Pop recalled. "A good time to go overseas. I was in the occupation forces and I got a three-month paid vacation. Oh, I saw plenty of fighting, all right. Booze fighting, I called it. Those Cubans could make the darndest things out of that sugar cane. The pay was fifteen dollars a month and we slept on the wet ground and ate beans, spuds, and embalmed beef.

"I really wasn't much of a soldier. Didn't know the meaning of discipline. I joined up to fight and they put me to marching and tried to teach me how to shoot. Made me mad. I could already knock the eye out of a squirrel in a pecan tree. Well, they got me out on the target range and gave me one of those old Springfields, the kind you could stick your thumb down the barrel. I raised up like I was shootin' a rabbit on the run and let fly at that target. Kick? Man, that old Springfield was dangerous at both ends."

Pop came home from Cuba and settled down on the farm and started following the mule around the corn patch. For years he was convinced the most foolish thing he ever did was volunteer for the Spanish-American fracas. "I always told my boys, I said, 'Boys, if they ever have another war, take to the woods.'"

For long lean years on the farm Pop refused to take a pension for his war service, because he figured nobody owed him a cent. But he finally got sick and had to take it, and now he considers joining the army the smartest thing he ever did.

The measure of local fame that reached Pop Brymer was not, however, the result of his being an old soldier. But rather for being an old dancer. When he was about sixty he thought he was getting old. Got to feeling bad and going to doctors. One day the doctor told him, "Pop, there's not anything the matter with you. What you need to do is quit digging ditches and start living. Go fishing, go dancing. Get out with the young people a little and stay away from the old folks."

Pop took the doctor seriously. At age sixty he'd never danced a step in his life. But he went out and learned. And for more than twenty years, he and Mrs. Brymer frequented the night spots over a wide area of Southeast Texas.

Doing the waltz or a nice fox trot?

"Heck no," Pop told me. "We do the jitterbug. Plenty of good exercise in that jitterbugging, and I recommend it for keeping healthy."

Pop's dancing days are about over, but he figures the jitterbugging added nearly a quarter of a century to his span. He's not so well now, but the last time I saw him he was still showing the jitterbug spirit, at least, the sharp sense of humor that made him a favorite of thousands of people that used to watch for him and Mrs. Brymer at the Saturday-night country dances. He turned on his little grin and said he'd been having a little trouble with his false teeth making his gums sore.

"The doctor told me that whiskey was good for treating

sore gums. Said just use it as a mouthwash and spit it out. I tried it awhile, but I finally quit it."

I asked did he mean he quit using whiskey as a mouth-wash?

"Naw," he said, "I mean I quit spittin' it out."

CHAPTER 6

"Tenaha, Timpson, Bobo and Blair."
—Dice-shooting soldiers
of Fory's Fusileers

It isn't likely that very many people outside Texas ever heard of Round Top, but to my notion it's among the cities in my state really worth visiting. And it is a city, duly incorporated since 1877, though the population stands at 124. It's in north Fayette County on State Highway 237.

First of all, there's the look of the place—a sort of inviting, village-type look. It has the square with the white frame town hall in the middle and the business houses lined up on just two sides. If it weren't for the fire station there'd be nothing but residences on the other two sides.

One of the houses on the square belongs to Mayor Don Nagel, and I remember the first day I called on him, in 1957, he came out from under a car he was repairing. Runs a garage and a service station across the highway from his house. He's a big dark-haired, round-featured, gruff-speaking fellow, and one of the hardest-working mayors I know anywhere. If Round Top had a million citizens he couldn't be prouder of his town.

Nagel washed the grease off his hands that day and we walked across the highway to his house, where he rummaged around and came up with an old and dog-eared envelope. It contained Round Top's original city charter, issued in 1877, written in longhand and signed by the

Texas secretary of state. Nagel read a little from the document. "The mayor and the town council shall have the power within the town to license and regulate billiard tables, tippling houses and dram shops." The charter also provides that it is unlawful in Round Top to fire a pistol or hit a man with the fist or stand in the doorway of a store in such a way as to interrupt business. And it specifies that the salary of the mayor shall not exceed $100 a year, which has turned out to be an unnecessary precaution because Mayor Nagel doesn't receive a cent of salary. "The city has only two paid employees," the mayor said. "One of them is the city marshal, who is paid sixty dollars a year, plus a two-dollar fee every time he makes an arrest. The other is the city secretary, who gets ten dollars a year."

The city marshal, Ernst Emmrich, came to see the mayor on a matter of business that first day I was in town. I wondered how much extra money he makes, above his base salary of sixty dollars a year, from the two-dollar arrest fee. "I make three or four arrests a year," he said.

To confirm this, Mayor Nagel hauled out an old legal-looking book—the *Mayor's Docket of Round Top*. If you happen to fire a pistol in town or hit a man with the fist or stand in the doorway of a store in such a way as to interrupt business, you may get arrested by Marshal Emmrich and armed immediately over to the house of Mayor Nagel. The mayor will wash the grease off his hands, hold court on the spot, and pronounce judgment. This is necessary because Round Top doesn't have a jail. It did at one time, but the town council decided that so few people got put in the thing it wasn't really needed. So the jail was torn down.

The first case ever recorded on the Mayor's Docket shows that a fellow hit a man with his fist in 1893 and was fined one dollar plus two dollars court costs. A more recent case involved a traveler who happened to pass through town. Round Top as a rule treats travelers handsomely, but this fellow was passing through at a speed that Marshal Emmrich estimated to be a hundred miles per hour. The reason he was arrested, he ran his car about three-quarters the way up a telephone pole, whereupon the marshal apprehended him, took him over to the house of Mayor Nagel, who fined him $9.95—one of the highest penalties ever set by a mayor's court.

Nagel explained that since Marshal Emmrich doesn't make many arrests he has extra duties which include assessing and collecting city taxes. This assures that he earns that five-dollar-a-month salary he is paid.

I asked the mayor how much money Round Top city taxes bring into the treasury. He said $185 a year. "After the two city employees are paid, we use the rest of the money to keep up the streets and maintain our four street lights."

When taxes don't bring in enough money to do justice to the budget, which is every year, the Round Top Do Your Duty Club gets busy. The DYD Club's membership includes everybody in town. All manner of fund-raising activities are held in the town hall, and this brings in a lot more money than taxes do. Besides, everybody has a dandy time at the DYD Club functions, which is better than paying taxes.

Nagel took me on a little tour of his city that day, as he has several times since. We went down in the deep and chilly basement of the old brewery building just off the square. The brewery doesn't operate any longer. Round Top once had a couple of cigar factories and a furniture shop and two hundred fifty people. It still has a beautiful Lutheran church built in 1866. We went in the church to see the organ, a truly remarkable instrument, handmade by one T. Wandtke a century ago. It's a hand-pump organ and it still operates nicely. The Rev. A. B. Weiss came out of the parsonage across the way and we climbed up in the choir loft. With Mayor Nagel on the pump, the preacher rendered a few bars of a hymn, and apologized and said the organ sounded a lot better on Sundays when Mrs. Roy Klump played it with her son Ronnie doing the pumping.

We inspected the red truck of the Round Top Fire Department, which has nearly two hundred members— seventy-five more than the city has population. The reason for this apparent oddity is that many farmers outside the city limits are members. Round Top is, of course, a farming community, and most of the people in the area are of German descent, good hard-working frugal farmers, and if you ever make a friend of one of them you've got a friend for life.

At Alderman Herman Birkelbach's Cafe we had turkey stew, and we visited at the Round Top State Bank with the cashier, George Frickie. Nagel asked the cashier if the city had any money in the bank. "Not much," he said.

But it didn't matter, because if the city suddenly needed money for anything, the Do Your Duty Club would hold a bingo game in the town hall and raise it.

Well, that's how things were in Round Top in 1957. Today they're different, but not much. The chief difference is that Houston people discovered Round Top. I knew they would sooner or later, because Houston money creeps steadily out of the big city and buys up farms and restores old houses for weekend retreats. It has bought not only a lot of farm land in the Round Top area but some of the old homes right in town and even some of the business houses, like the old brewery and Emil Schwarz's Grocery Store. In a very short space of time, Round Top began to look pretty sprucy, with new coats of white paint on buildings and restored homes, and a lot of city folks running in and out of town on weekends and in summer.

A country town views the coming of the city folks with mixed feeling. Business around town improves some, and elderly people with farms or quaint homes have a chance to unload their property for a good price and acquire a little pot of gold to pay doctor bills. But it's tough for local people to keep from resenting the invasion. They like their little communities the way they were, and have a good bit to say in private about the "new people," though not all of it is uncomplimentary. This is a situation faced by many, many little communities in Texas now which stand within weekend driving distance of the cities.

However, sometimes the little towns don't change as much as the local people think, or as much as outside observers believe. In 1964 I went to Round Top's big Fourth-of-July celebration, the big event of any year in that proud little place. If the city folks had managed to change that celebration, then I figured Round Top's metamorphosis would be complete.

Well, they haven't changed anything. Not on the Fourth of July. When the country people in the area come to town, the city folks fade into oblivion and insignificance.

A July 4 celebration at Round Top is in the old tradition. It consists simply of a short round of speeches and a parade in the morning, a mighty barbecue eating and beer drinking at noon, a baseball game at 3 P.M., and a big dance in the "Hall" that night. It had been a long time since I'd stood out in the hot sun on the Fourth of July and listened to a patriotic speech, and I tell you there's something inspiring about it. You fan and you sweat and you suffer a little, and then when the flag comes by at the head of the parade you can recapture that old full feeling in the breast when you salute it. A curious thing, that a community of people most of whose forebears lie buried back in Germany have taught so many visitors to regain the old spirit of the Fourth of July, a holiday that has degenerated in the cities to a day of loafing around the house.

One little scene at that celebration convinced me that no amount of millionaires will ever change Round Top completely. It had to do with beer drinking. Like all German towns, Round Top loves its beer and drinks it openly like youngsters down red soda water. As the parade made the square—there aren't many streets, so the procession just went round and round the square—every second spectator stood in the sun with a bottle in his hand, and nobody considered it crude or in bad taste. I'll not forget the sight of one hefty local citizen who was providing a chair for one of the honor guests at the celebration, a grand and kindly and cultured lady out of the city. While performing the courtesy of placing this wealthy lady's chair in a shady spot where she could view the parade, the fellow had a bottle of beer in his hand. And once the guest was seated and her benefactor had bent down to inquire as to her comfort, he straightened up, took a deep draft out of the bottle, stretched his neck, and patted his ample middle a time or two to control the belch forming there. What an eloquent gesture, which, translated into words, meant, "The lady is comfortable, and we are ready. Let the celebration begin."

Now Round Top isn't the smallest incorporated city in Texas. There's Kirvin, in Freestone County, which isn't the smallest either, but it only has two taxpayers.

I drove to Kirvin one afternoon and called on Mayor O. A. Carter, who can see just about every house in the city limits from his front porch. Here's how the conversation went:

What's the population of Kirvin now?

"About eighty-nine," the mayor said, "near as I can figure. Haven't counted up lately."

What form of city government does Kirvin have?

"Well, mayor and city commission. Two members on the commission—the postmaster and the Methodist preacher. Postmaster's also city treasurer."

Is the treasury in pretty good shape?

"I think there's about thirty-six dollars in it now."

What's the tax rate?

"Well, nobody here in town pays any taxes. Now we do have two taxpayers. A pipe-line company that has a line running through the townsite, and then the railroad, and they pay up faithfully, too. Don't even have to send 'em a notice."

But does this provide enough revenue to operate the city?

"No, but the county commissioner keeps up the streets, and if we need money for anything else we just put a notice up over in Wynn's grocery and everybody in town contributes a little, whatever they can afford."

What's this money used for?

"Mowing, mostly. In wet seasons the Johnson grass grows up pretty thick all over town. It gets too bad, we put up the notice and pretty soon we've got enough money to pay a man to mow."

How many businesses in the city?

"Just the one yonder—Wynn's Grocery and Feed."

Does the city commission meet regularly?

"Well, there's been I believe two meetings since I've been mayor."

How long has that been?

"Four years."

Is there any advantage in a community of eighty-nine people being incorporated?

"We think it helps hold the people together, and that's important to us. And it keeps the churches open, too. We've lost our public school here, and when you lose your school your community falls apart if you don't do something to hold it. And it keeps up spirit. For instance there was a man here few years ago got burned out. House was ruined. Lost everything he had. Well, we put up the notice at Wynn's and more than three hundred dollars was raised to help the man. And with the things people gave him, he had more household furnishings after the fire than before."

Country towns die hard. A place like Kirvin may avoid complete obscurity for another half century, but it seems certain to disappear one day and be forgotten. Other little Texas communities are never forgotten because they have something to be famous for. This often keeps a town's name on people's tongues for decades even after it has died.

For example, if you judge notoriety by the number of times the name of a place is spoken, the likelihood is that the most famous towns in Texas are Tenaha, Timpson, Bobo, and Blair. The reason for this is that there are so many dice players in the world. When trying to make ten with dice, crap shooters everywhere are apt to holler Tenaha, Timpson, Bobo, and Blair, even though they may not even know what the words mean. These four towns are strung out along U.S. 59 in the East Texas county of Shelby.

Now how in creation did four little places in East Texas ever get to be so common on the tongues of dice players? I once set out to try to solve that mystery. At Tenaha, Bobo, and Blair I found no one who could shed any light on the matter. Blair, now, is more of a rural neighborhood than a

town. It centers around a white frame church and a ceme-
tery on the Attoyac Bayou a short drive off Highway 59.
And Bobo, which was once a humming railpoint, now consists chiefly of a service station and grocery store on Flat
Fork Creek. At Tenaha (popularly pronounced Tennyhaw)
there's still plenty of civilization—or at least about as much
as eleven hundred citizens could be expected to produce,
and Timpson is very little bigger. People in Shelby County
make their living mainly from chicken raising and pine timber production but they will never raise anything that will
put any of their towns on the map like crapshooters have
put Tenaha, Timpson, Bobo, and Blair.

At Timpson, I located R. R. Morrison, Colonel, U. S. Army
(ret.), who said the old dice shooter's cry had its beginning
right there in town just before World War I. Morrison was
then captain of a local company of infantry organized as
Fory's Fusileers, named in honor of a Timpson railroad
agent, H. R. Fory. The Fusileers later became Company B,
3rd Texas Infantry, of the National Guard, and Colonel
Morrison led the company to France in World War I.

Just before leaving home the infantrymen in that company had a few dice games, as soldiers anywhere are apt to
do before going overseas, or even when they're coming
home, for that matter. Anyway, while talking to the dice as
crapshooters do and calling on them to make ten, one of
the boys happened to yell, "Tenny-haw!" Which inspired
another, who was apparently betting his friend would make
the point, to answer with "Timpson!" and somebody else
threw in Bobo and Blair. This was a natural thing, for the
four towns lay within a few miles of each other along the
railroad and passengers were accustomed to hearing the
stations called in that order. And it made a nice alliterative
phrase, pleasing as it rolled off the tongue.

The names of the soldiers who applied this cry to crap

[108]

shooting will remain forever a mystery, but the fact is clear that the phrase sailed to Europe with Fory's Fusileers. There it fell on fertile ground and spread to dice games the world over. During World War II in Europe I heard dice players from New York and Pennsylvania, Ohio, Nevada, and California and various other states invoking the dice to make ten in the names of Tenaha, Timpson, Bobo, and Blair, but I never found one who'd believe me when I explained that those are the names of four small towns in Shelby County, Texas.

Some little burgs are worth stopping in just because they have a good sense of humor. I have a great fondness for such places. The citizens of these towns refuse to take themselves very seriously, with the result that they have a dandy lot of fun just getting up in the morning and walking around town and being alive. I've often tried without any success to figure out why it is that some towns have fun all the time while others of the same size and similar background sit around all long-faced, talking about their ancestors and how much better things were in the old days.

In Wharton County there's a town called Louise. Has 882 citizens. Even the chamber of commerce of Louise has a sense of humor. This is pretty astonishing, because most chambers of commerce in towns of that size view themselves with an awesome seriousness.

Ralph Stockton, who is just a guy you meet when you go to Louise, explained to me with a straight face, "When we organized a chamber of commerce we wanted to put up a clean front, so we elected Baldy Crowell president because he's the only man in town who takes a bath and shaves every morning. Besides, he's got the only air-conditioned office in town and it makes a good place to meet. Paul Sablatura, our county commissioner, introduces Baldy at the chamber-of-commerce meetings as the past, present, and future president, and for a slogan we adopted 'Leave It To Baldy.'"

This slogan is printed in boldface type in the local telephone directory and would be expensive to change if anybody else got Crowell's position, so he seems in office to stay. But if Louise had a city charter and a local government, which it doesn't, the mayor would be Sablatura. As county commissioner, he keeps all the streets paved and the vacant lots mowed, and nobody has to pay city taxes for these services. But in addition to that Sablatura is a good musician and entertainer, and so is handy to have around at special occasions like celebrations. He works without any pay, just the same as Crowell does. Crowell, along with his brother Bo, is a driller of water wells, and both of them distribute business cards that say, "Help Stamp Out Windmills."

There's always something a little different, amusing or interesting or offbeat, going on around Louise that makes life interesting there. Small things, sometimes, that you may discover just by walking into Raymond Hillyer's Grocery Store. The difference I found between going into Hillyer's and going into a grocery store in the city was that at the check-out stand Mrs. Lucille Rutledge had a fruit jar sitting by the cash register with a big green worm in it. This was being displayed for the amazement of the customers. It was a beautiful worm. He had spots all over him in various brilliant colors—yellow, green, blue, orange. You wouldn't find a prettier worm anywhere, and in Louise it seemed right and proper that it be exhibited at the grocer's.

Ralph Stockton always claimed that, since Louise is not big enough to afford a full-time town drunk, various of the men around town take turns filling the role, so the job won't be too hard on any one fellow's constitution. Well, of course you know that isn't true, just the same as it's not true that M. W. (Baldy) Crowell is the only man in town that shaves every morning. All the same I find it refreshing in contrast to the overabundance of little towns that are sick with pride and self-importance and that might, if anybody suggested it, issue a straight-faced news release announcing that the town doesn't have a single drunk and that all the men shave and bathe every day.

Visitors to Louise are generally taken over to the mill and presented with a sack of brown rice. The town is located in the heart of the Texas rice belt, and Ralph Stockton maintains that all its citizens eat this unpolished rice. "That's how it's eaten over in China," Stockton says, "where the men live to be a hundred and become fathers every year." Stockton has not been able to explain why it is, then, that Louise has a population of no more than 882.

Among the notable things at Louise is its newspaper, which is the biggest in Texas, and maybe in the world. That is, if you judge it by page size and not circulation. A page of this newspaper measures eight by sixteen feet, and if that sounds to you like a billboard, you are right. This outdoor newspaper stands beside a small drive-in grocery on U.S. 59. The editor is Tillie Roome, who works in the grocery store. When she hears a piece of news, she runs out to the billboard with a piece of chalk and writes it up. Anybody that wants to catch up on the news, then, just drives by the grocery store and reads it, without even getting out of the car.

Tillie Roome has a press card issued by the Texas Department of Public Safety to prove she is a newspaper editor. The news she deals in includes such items as who is in the hospital and who has had a baby, and who is valedictorian at the high school, and other school and church announcements. If there's no fresh news, the editor just changes the date and lets the same news run that ran the day before. There is no charge for advertising, and you will find offered in the classified section a Toulouse goose and twelve goslings and similar bargains.

Baldy Crowell, in addition to being chamber-of-commerce president, is fishing editor of the outdoor newspaper. In one edition I read, Crowell had reported that the trout were biting live shrimp at Half Moon Reef in Matagorda Bay, a few miles south on the coast. Some fisherman, apparently having taken Baldy's advice, had returned empty-creeled to scrawl a comment alongside Crowell's report, indicating it wasn't worth the chalk it took to write it.

Now that is the beautiful thing about having an outdoor newspaper. Any reader that doesn't agree with what he reads can just come along and write in a rebuttal.

Madisonville is a little like Louise in that not just a whole lot ever happens there, so that when anything does it's a great occasion. Two big events occur in Madisonville annually—one is the Sidewalk Cattlemen's Barbecue and the other is when the bees swarm out of the walls of the courthouse.

The seat of Madison County's government is a red brick, white-trimmed courthouse that probably would have been torn down and replaced a long time ago if the local people could bear to part with it. I doubt they could. The courthouse is a venerable old party that seems remarkably suited to the personality of the town. One of the ways in which it is different from other courthouses is that its walls are infested with honeybees. They've been hived up there for nearly forty years. In summer the county office workers who sit by open windows are often dive-bombed by the bees, which are also pests in other ways. For example, a few years ago when the county decided to paint the courthouse belfry, a bee expert instead of a painter had to be employed because no professional painter cared to go up there and risk the wrath of those insects.

But there has been no serious effort to remove those bees, and I suspect the reason is that Madisonville has too much fun with them. Every spring the bees swarm out of the walls and congregate on a limb of one of the cottonwood trees on the lawn. Then a mighty competition is held, to see who has the fortitude and the skill to capture a free colony of honeybees without getting stung sick. Business activity slows to a crawl at such times and a great crowd lines the courthouse square to watch the action—though it is inclined to watch from a safe distance, calling out encouragement and useless advice to those engaged in the battle.

One afternoon I climbed up in the tower of that courthouse with Dave Morgan, the janitor. Not to investigate the bees, for those I'll be happy to leave to the brave, but to satisfy a longing I had from boyhood to wind a courthouse clock. Madison County's courthouse is one of the few remaining in Texas with a weight-driven clock in it. To get up in the tower, you climb several sets of cobweb-draped stairs that look like the ones you see in horror movies, and the wind leaking into that tower sets up a lot of noisy creaking and provides a very ghosty effect.

Two huge weights hang from cables in that tower—one weight moves slowly down to provide the power to drive the clock, and the other drives the striking bell. Once a week Morgan goes up there to crank the weights up, and it's a pretty good job requiring some muscle.

Many of these old weight-driven clocks have been electrified now, because the weights constitute a threat to the safety of people in the courthouse. At Bellville, county seat of Austin County, one night a cable in the winding system parted and one of the weights—about two thousand pounds' worth—crashed down through the roof of the district court-room and wrecked the place. Shortly before that happened a meeting was being held in that courtroom, but fortunately the people had all left before the weight fell. At any rate this incident led Austin County to electrify its courthouse clock and get rid of the weights, leaving Madison County with the only weight-driven courthouse clock that I know of in my part of Texas.

Courthouse clock towers are fun to roam around in, until the clock strikes. It knocks your ears off, and my suggestion is, don't go up there until after twelve noon unless you want to be deafened. But a public clock has a great deal of appeal to local people, and once they get accustomed to it they often refuse to part with one. At Hempstead, when a new Waller County courthouse was built, a modern IBM clock system was installed, but Hempstead people complained so much about missing the sound of the courthouse clock chimes that the old bells were reinstalled.

The four faces of the clock in the Madison County court-house have looked down on some pretty woolly incidents, in the times when street fights and shootings were common and a lot of guys got thrown in the horse trough after being knocked cold. Once a year Madisonville goes back to throwing people in the horse trough, one of which is yet maintained on the corner of the square. Sponsor of this chicanery is the Madisonville Sidewalk Cattlemen's Association, which sets forth rules pertaining to the wearing of cowboy boots in town. If a man walks on the streets in Madisonville during the week of the Sidewalk Cattlemen's annual celebration, he had better own cows if he wears boots or he may get heaved in the horse trough as penalty.

This celebration provides an insight into the nature of small-town Texas men. Shows what sort of entertainment they enjoy. What they enjoy immensely is exchanging friendly insults. At a banquet held in connection with this celebration and attended by almost every male citizen in Madisonville, the speaker spent an hour insulting the community's leaders.

The county judge and the mayor were accused of misappropriating public funds; an insurance man was said to have knocked a cracked window out of his office to collect on an insurance policy he sold himself; an oilman was held up as a widow cheater; a cattleman was called a rustler; a church worker said to be a heavy drinker, and so on. On such occasions the hero of the evening is the man whose character, after all the insults have been delivered and appraised, has been painted the blackest. And the only ones who really feel insulted are those not insulted at all and so feel left out.

This sort of horseplay is by no means confined to Madisonville. I've sat in dozens of luncheon meetings with the Lions and Rotary and Kiwanis and similar clubs, and heard a hundred bankers called embezzlers from the speaker's rostrum, and I've not ever seen a banker so insulted do anything but sit back and beam about it.

CHAPTER 7

"Cuz, this fool car's runnin' away with us."
—Welcome Woods

At Millican, a once-bustling but now near dormant community in south Brazos County, I stopped one warm morning and asked a woman standing by the railroad crossing who was the best storyteller in town.

"Well," she said, "that would be L. R. Thompson, lives over yonder on the hill. But there's no use in going over there this time of day. Mr. Thompson works from dawn till dark and won't stop to talk to anybody until he gets done with what he's working on."

I figured anybody who works that much ought to be worth meeting, so I followed directions to Thompson's house to see if he was really so dedicated to his labors.

He was working, all right. Pumping up a tire on his car. I stopped at the front gate and called, in the accepted custom of the country. Thompson was obviously a little displeased at this interruption, but he laid the pump down and walked out to the gate. A small fellow, well up in years, with a serious, unsmiling face almost hidden by a wide-brimmed hat. For about fifteen seconds he stood here and listened to me before he interrupted.

"Yes, I could tell you some yarns, but I'm too busy. I could tell you about the race riots and the tragic baptizing on the Brazos and the massacre at the section house. I'm the only one left alive around here that remembers the mas-

[116]

sacre at the section house. But the roof on my house is leaking and when I get through fixing that I've got to start painting." He turned as if to go back to his tire pumping.

I asked if I couldn't come in the yard and just stand around and listen while he worked.

"No," he said. "I'll be up on that roof. Come back when I'm not busy."

Well, that was a disappointment. I'd heard about the massacre at the Millican section house. Supposed to be a real hairy yarn, and I wanted to hear it from an authority. The woman back at the railroad crossing had said Thompson was a boy in his teens when it happened, in the middle 1890s. That would make him around eighty at the time I called on him, and here he was still crawling up on roofs, pumping up tires, and painting houses.

Suddenly he changed his mind. "I'll take time," he said, "to tell you just one story."

He told it standing there at the gate, and he told it fast.

"This is about the tragic baptizing on the Brazos. It happened in the summer of 1836."

I'd have preferred the massacre at the section house but decided I'd better not argue.

"The settlers around here had just returned from the Runaway Scrape, during the Texas Revolution," Thompson said, "when they took a notion to hold a big camp meeting. So they all collected at Richtor Rocks, down the river from here a way. Every settler in the country was there. They built a brush arbor and the camp meeting lasted three weeks. There were thirty-five converts. I got the story from an aunt of mine. She was seven years old then and she attended that camp meeting.

"Well, they were going to baptize the converts in the river there at Richtor Rocks. So the preacher waded out and went through the preliminaries and then three of the penitents were passed out to him in the water for baptizing.

"Now listen and get this straight. The fourth convert was a girl, sixteen years old. The preacher dipped her under and she slipped out of his hands. He grabbed for her but couldn't reach her. Everybody on the bank commenced to get excited. The young men all jumped in the water and tried to find the girl. She didn't come up, though, and all her family there on the bank were crying and carrying on.

"After a time the preacher raised his hands and commanded silence. 'The Lord giveth and the Lord taketh away,' he said. 'Blessed be the name of the Lord. Now fetch out another one.'

"Well, there were thirty-one converts standing there on the riverbank, but not a one of them would wade out to be baptized. And do you know that girl's body was never found. The supposition was that an alligator got her. Now I've got to get back to work."

So back to work he went, striding purposefully toward the car and the flat tire and the pump, leaving me standing there at the gate.

I just wish that good Texas storytellers were as easy to find as the public insists. People are misled in this regard by what they see. When they drive across Texas in summer, they notice small groups of elderly men sitting out in front of highway stores. Motorists imagine for some reason that all these old gents are good storytellers, and that if you stopped awhile and sat with them they would regale you with fascinating yarns from out of the past, their speech spiced with delightful rural sayings and homely philosophies.

It isn't so.

Still the mass of city Texans insists it is. Say a friend rides with me across a couple hundred miles of Texas. We pass a country store and view The Scene—that is, the most common of rural scenes in this state that motorists take notice of—the group of overalled elderly men on the benches. The friend always says, jerking his thumb at The Scene, "I'd give a dollar to sit in on that conversation awhile. Man, a guy in your business could sit there for three hours and just listen and he'd have material for a book."

The greater likelihood is that if a stranger walked into that group, the conversation would cease, or at least tail off into a series of short mumbled comments and grunted answers. I have traveled my state over for a good many years with an ear bent for storytellers, and my experience is that you find mighty few of them just by accident. I know of few places I can now go and feel certain of hearing good rural conversation that's worth recording.

As for the old guys in the overalls sitting out front of the country store, perhaps it will be a service to tell the public what they are talking about. I know, at least, what they are most likely to be discussing. It will be the land, and what's happened to the price of it since World War II.

Because most of the old gents you see along the road are displaced farmers. Displaced, at least, in that they no longer farm because somebody came along and bought their land. Or because they are too old to farm. Or because the kind of farming they know isn't profitable any longer.

The land is surely and not so slowly passing from the hands of small farmers into that of the bigger ones, and into the hands of city buyers with that deep yearning for life in the country. They buy the land for twice the price a man could pay if he planned to wrest a living from it. They put up pretty country homes with porches overlooking small lakes. They remodel old barns and paint them red and stick weathervanes on the roofs. And erect a sign by the front gate—"Happy Acres."

This is what the old men talk about. About how they bought land in 1910 for two dollars an acre, sold it in 1946 for ninety. And how the man that bought from them sold it for a hundred twenty dollars, and now last week it resold for two hundred fifty. They talk of this because it's the most spectacular thing that's happened in their lifetimes.

But enough of country economics. I mention it only in what will be, I know, an unsuccessful attempt to dispel the notion that the clutches of old men sitting by the sides of Texas roads, or around the stoves in winter, are just waiting for somebody to come along and listen to them spin delightful yarns. The best storytellers I've found had to be stalked, like game.

Well, now you do run into a lot of just plain talkers. These are not often storytellers, but sometimes they come close.

Bob Michael, for example.

One afternoon a friend and I were driving south down the state between Dallas and Houston, pulled off at Mexia for a cold drink. The establishment was similar to thousands of others you find sitting beside Texas highways. A few tables and chairs, a pool table, a row of stools, and a counter. From behind the counter are dispensed soft drinks and beer and sandwiches and hard-boiled eggs and pickled wieners and little slabs of cheese. When my friend was served his drink, he reached for one of the pickled wieners.

"You're just like me," a big fellow from behind the counter said. "When you drink something, you've got to eat. Now I don't drink beer, but when I drink a soda pop I'll generally get me a package of these little crackers."

The speaker was Michael, a leather-skinned man in his sixties whom we'd never before seen. He leaned on the counter and watched with approval as my friend consumed the pickled wiener and pronounced it good. Clearly, Michael wanted to talk, so we assumed listening expressions and let him fly. This is what he said:

"I bet I can say something not many other folks can say. I can say I've worked in beer joints for twenty years and never had one swallow of beer. Never even tasted the stuff. Don't know why. Just never got started. Now I've been around folks all my life that got drunk a lot and did some bootleggin', too, but I just never started it and I'm glad I didn't.

"And I'll tell you what. I was able to keep work and do better on account of it. When all these others around here were makin' thirty-five and forty dollars a week I was makin' fifty and sixty and for a long time even seventy dollars.

"Now some of 'em tell me, 'Well, Bob, you should have been a preacher, not drinkin' and all.' But I say no, I'm too mean for that. I've pulled many a beer. I guess I've pulled more bottles of beer than any man in this county, and never drank one. No, and not any whiskey, either, or anything with alcohol.

"The way I got started working in this place, I used to be a ball player and a coon hunter, and I shot my hand and arm all up. You see how it crippled this right hand. I couldn't go to the field and pick cotton, so one day a man and his wife ran a place wanted some help and I went to work for 'em. That was twenty years ago and I been at it ever since.

"Man runs a place like this, he likes a helper doesn't drink. You've got to watch things. And I know who the drunks are and who the minors are, and I know how to watch things. You've got to watch everything in a place like this. Other day I came in here and looked around and I noticed a cigarette lighter was missing from that display card there. And I told John, that's the fellow owns this place, I said, 'John, I see you sold a cigarette lighter.' Well, he hadn't either sold one, and hadn't noticed one missing. I knew it was a $3.95 lighter, so then he checked to see if the sale was rung up on the cash register. And it wasn't. And I knew who took that lighter, too. You got to watch.

"Couple fellows came in here other day, couple just about like you fellows, and one of 'em reached in this jar here and got a package of crackers and ate 'em. Then he commenced dickerin' for a set of them big steer horns John's got for sale up there. Asked how much they were.

"I said fifteen dollars. John'd told me what to get for 'em. Well, the fellow said John'd told him the horns weren't but ten dollars. I said no, they were fifteen. Well, he commenced to get mad about it. He said, 'Why you . . . I could buy and sell you a hundred times.' And I said, 'I guess you could 'cause I ain't got nothin', but if you're so danged rich how about payin' for that nickel package of crackers you ate?'

"No, the way I got this hand ruined, I was coon huntin'. That was twenty-two years ago. Dogs'd treed a coon and I set my shotgun down in a holler stump. When I went to pick it up I hit the trigger and I shot myself. Blood? Blood flyin' all over the place. You could see them two arm bones there astickin' out. I thought I'd killed myself. I said to my brother that was with me, I said, 'Well, I've killed myself.'

"But I walked a mile back to the house and come out of it all right. There's still thirty-five Number Four shot in this leg, ten in this arm, and one up here in my cheek. Well, here comes John."

When John came in, his helper left. After that things sure were quiet.

About once a year I stop at Milano just to see what J. L. Hayman has to say. Generally it's plenty. Hayman is a big fellow past middle age who moves slow but steady, and he has a way of talking in a low-pitched monotone that somehow makes you lean forward and listen.

Hayman, among various other things, is a beekeeper. My observation has been that beekeepers most often are remarkably independent, free-thinking men. I never met a beekeeper that didn't have strong opinions on politics and government and in fact on all matters.

A visitor is likely to find Hayman moving around his premises in overalls and a leather cap and a three-day beard. One afternoon he sat in the doorway of his work-shop, with one foot bare to air out a sore toe he had at the time. Got to talking about how he quit smoking cigarettes.

"I knew cigarettes were hurtin' me, and my imagination bein' what it is, I got to picturin' what a lung cancer looked like. I could see that thing growin' right here in my left lung and it was about the size and shape of an egg just after you break it in the skillet. Then, too, I got to thinkin' what kind of a lookin' corpse I'd make in the casket.

"Now, the natural inclination of a man is to think, well, I'll quit soon's I finish this pack I'm smokin' now. But then he's apt to reach for another pack. What you have to do is get mad at half a pack of cigarettes. I took that half pack and twisted it, like this, and tore it up and rubbed it between my hands and made a wasp nest out of it and chunked it in the garbage can. Then I made two rules. First one, I said I'd never put another cigarette in my mouth. And the second rule, I said if I did, I wouldn't light it. Well, that was six years ago and I haven't broken the first rule yet.

"Now I did gain weight. Got up to a hundred and ninety

and then two hundred and then two ten, and then I quit weighin'. I told the doctor the other day, I said the only reason I'm sorry I quit smokin' is, I can smell so many rotten things I couldn't smell before."

Pausing scarcely a second to change gears, Hayman shifted from cigarettes to the federal government, one of his favorite subjects. Or targets.

"The beekeepers of Texas have had to kick these government do-gooders in the teeth two or three times to keep 'em out of the honey business, spending our tax dollars. Did you ever hear how these fellows work that trap monkeys for a living? Well, they use a jar that's secured on the ground. The procedure is to put some bait down in the jar and then scatter some more around on the outside, free samples that the monkeys can eat. That's the taxpayers' dollars. But the monkey loses his freedom when he sticks his hand in that jar. He can't draw it out with his fist doubled up, and he's too greedy to turn the bait loose and pull his hand out and regain his freedom and his dignity and his self-reliance. He's like the farmer that came home with a big old rattlesnake, and his wife asked him, 'Mack, what you gonna do with that thing?' And the farmer said, 'I don't know, but a fella was giving 'em away.'"

We went out in Hayman's bee yard awhile to watch those remarkable insects at work. Hayman can generally find some aspect of a bee's behavior to illustrate his philosophies. Simple and old-fashioned tenets such as, "If you're not gonna work, get out." We stood in front of a big hive of Italian bees. Dozens of them were congregated on the narrow landing board at the hive entrance.

"Notice," Hayman said, "those guard bees there on the edge of the landing board. Their business is to keep out bees that don't have any business in the hive. When a bee comes flyin' in over his head, that guard bee sort of rears up on his hind legs and sniffs at the newcomer. He wants to be sure that bee belongs. If he doesn't, all the guard bees will flat tear him up and throw him out.

"Now look there, right now, on the landing board. See those two bees tryin' to push a third one out on the ground? What that is, it's an old bee and they want to get rid of 'im. They're sayin', 'Bud, you're just eatin' and not workin' and you've got to go.' They'll whip 'im half to death with their wings and push 'im off the board. Then if he's able he'll try to crawl back up in the hive. After he crawls back a time or two a couple of 'em will grab hold and fly off with him, carry him maybe far as from here to the house, and drop him. Then they'll say, 'OK, Bud, let's see you crawl back from there.'"

Among Hayman's enterprises at Milano were a service station and a café. When Congress passed the civil rights law, with its strong public accommodations provisions, Hayman thought his own civil rights were being violated. Nobody was going to tell him who he could or couldn't serve. So he sold out—café, service station, and all—and walked away.

That café was the sort that most travelers, passing through Texas, don't stop at. They hurry on to the next city to eat, where they get fancier food but miss a lot of fun.

When Hayman had the café, the women who walked into it often got whistled at—one of those low, wolf-type whistles. The whistler was Jack, a black myna bird who lived there in Hayman's place for several years. Jack can talk enough to tell people what kind of bird he is, because that's the question people ask him most, and when he answers he then asks in return, "What kind of bird are *you?*" This always struck Hayman as a fair question and Jack seemed perplexed when nobody ever answered him.

[125]

This bird was mighty noisy in that café. He liked to remain quiet for a while and about the time a customer started sipping coffee he'd let fly with one of his piercing screams that'd knock the spoon out of a cup.

"But you know," Hayman said just before he sold the café, "I'm afraid Jack's gettin' a little old. I suspect his eyesight's gettin' a little dim. When he was a young bird a girl had to be an outstanding beauty for Jack to whistle at her. Lately I've noticed him whistlin' at some old snaggle-toothed chicks. Gettin' so when he whistles I don't even look up from my work."

Among those you may see in company with J. L. Hayman around Milano is Welcome Woods, a man well known in that region as a buyer and seller and trader of hogs. Folks say he can guess a hog's weight as close as a public scales. Also that he's got a heart the size of a washtub, that if he had all the money he's spent helping people out of financial difficulty he'd be living in the biggest house on Easy Street.

But in my view the highest praise to be heaped on Welcome Woods is that he is willing to tell a good yarn on himself and give a man permission to print it. The tale about his runaway car, for example.

Woods used to drive an old Model A Ford. Along with the man he calls Cuz—one of his true cousins—Welcome had driven the Ford into neighboring Robertson County on hog business and was driving home across the Brazos Bottom on U.S. 79. The night was dark and windy.

Now, it happened that two other Milano citizens—Harvin Reese and Alvin Nelson—were driving along the same highway, behind Welcome and Cuz. They recognized Welcome's car and hatched up a shenanigan. Nelson switched off his lights and eased up behind the old Ford. Both Nelson and Reese drove that road many times, and knew that just ahead a State Highway Department traffic counter lay stretched across the pavement. When a car rolled over that counter, the driver could feel a slight bump of his wheels.

With Reese out on the running board to guide him in a neat bit of timing, Nelson began pushing Welcome's Ford just as it bumped over the traffic counter. That's why Welcome and Cuz weren't aware of the nature of the strange force that gripped their little car that night.

Nelson picked up speed, pushing the Model A.

"I noticed she seemed to be runnin' a little fast at low throttle," Welcome says, "but I didn't think too much about it because the highway was downhill at that spot. So I just eased 'er out of gear and let 'er roll. But about a quarter mile later I could tell something was wrong. She began rollin' uphill well as down and was pickin' up speed to boot."

That was when Cuz began noticing that the telegraph poles were marching past mighty swiftly. His cousin was running a little fast, wasn't he?

Welcome agreed. He hit the brakes. The car kept speeding. He hit them again. Nothing happened. The unseen force behind was too great. What mysterious business could be going on here in the dark night, that a car gained speed when the brakes were applied?

"Cuz," Welcome said gravely, "this fool car's runnin' away with us."

Cuz didn't believe it. He figured the foot feed was stuck. He reached to the floor to unstick it and got his hand stomped by Welcome, who was still working on the brakes.

When Cuz came up from the floor board and looked at the speedometer, still climbing, he had a right to be concerned. For in his hand he held the accelerator, yanked out by the roots. And Welcome was clutching the wheel in a desperate steering battle.

He yelled, "What'll we do, Cuz?"

"Just hold 'er on the road," hollered Cuz. "Maybe she'll run out of gas."

"Thunder, man, she's got enough gas in 'er to carry us through Austin!"

Both Cuz and Welcome were shouting now, while the wind roared into the open windows and the car sped along faster than a Model A is supposed to go. So now they were approaching the little town of Gause, just west of the Brazos River.

"Cuz," Welcome shouted, "if we go through Gause at this speed we'll kill somebody. I'm gonna take 'er off across a field."

"You do that," Cuz argued desperately, "and you'll kill somebody anyway, and it'll be us. Cut the switch! Kill the motor!"

"The switch!" yelled Welcome. "Why, hell, man, I've had the switch off and the key in my pocket for the last mile and a half!"

Then Cuz remembered you could reach under the dash of a Model A, lean the carburetor down to zero, and cut off the gas supply. He managed to get that done. Still the car rolled on.

Back under the dash went Cuz. He grabbed what he could find and yanked. He came up with about five feet of wiring. No car could run without that vital wiring, yet Welcome's Ford rolled on.

Laughing witnesses to much of the frenzied action inside the Model A, Reese and Nelson in the car behind finally dropped back as they approached a railroad underpass near Gause. The Model A sailed through the underpass and began to slow down on the upgrade beyond. Both Welcome and Cuz hit the ditch on both sides of the highway, and the runaway car, doors flapping like a buzzard's wings, bounced off the highway and stopped at the top of the grade.

Nelson and Reese, car lights now blazing, pulled up and asked innocently if Welcome and Cuz were having some kind of trouble. They didn't get an answer. Who would believe what had happened?

Welcome gets a good belly laugh out of telling that story yet. I asked if it didn't occur to him to look back, to see if anything was pushing his car.

"It did when I'd been pushed about a mile," Welcome said. "And after that I was too busy."

When passing through the city of Lockhart, it's always worthwhile to stop and listen to J. Henry Martindale. He sits in a narrow office on the first floor of the Caldwell County Courthouse, where he is county treasurer. On his desk is a sign that says in big black letters, "Horse and Mule." It doesn't mean anything. It's just there to make people ask questions so Henry can then talk to them. He also has a sign on his desk that says smoking is prohibited, but I have counted as many as seven ash trays and five pipes in his office, and two of the pipes going at once.

You get accustomed to strange things after you visit Lockhart a few times. The early visits may prove confusing, though. For example I was an honor guest one day of the Plum Creek Luncheon Club of Lockhart. This pleased me a great deal because I'd not ever been an honor guest at anything before. The Luncheon Club meets eighteen times a week in a local café. It has no president, but every member is a vice-president. To qualify as a member, a man must agree to be opposed to rattlesnakes, flies, long speeches, and paper napkins. Also, though they call themselves a luncheon club, all the members go home for the noon meal and never, ever have a luncheon.

If you happen to pass through Lockhart and the Plum Creek Club invites you for coffee, which is the only thing you will get invited for, you may be perplexed at the difficulty you will have in sugaring your coffee. This will be because the spoon in the sugar bowl has got a big hole in it. Sometimes your coffee may be served, on the coldest day of the year, with ice in it. Or your water glass will leak. A fellow I know was having coffee with the club, when a waitress slithered up and whispered, "Sir, here is a note from the manager of the café." He opened the note to read, "Please wipe off your chin."

The day I was honor guest of the Plum Creek Club I was presented with a gold-headed walking cane, a beautiful thing. Well, I didn't quite get presented with it. One of the vice-presidents (I don't remember which because the club had thirty-eight at the time and all of equal standing) was making the presentation, extolling the merits of the walking cane. To show its sturdiness, he whacked it on the table smartly and the cane broke into four pieces. Then everybody got up and walked out.

The Plum Creek Luncheon Club is just one of several fascinating institutions around Lockhart. J. Henry Martindale, whom I started out to tell you about, is another. Martindale is a combination politician and journalist. In addition to serving as Caldwell County treasurer he writes a column for a Lockhart newspaper, and for years he served as local correspondent for two or three city dailies as well as for the wire services.

Back when he was attending Harmony Grove School, Martindale was exposed to the truism that confession is good for the soul. So he volunteered to tell me about the biggest boner he ever pulled as a newspaper correspondent.

"It was just before a Thanksgiving," he said, dragging on a pipe about as long as his arm, for J. Henry is a little old guy, "and the merchants around town turned a bunch of turkeys loose on the square, to draw a crowd into town. Whoever caught a turkey could keep it, you know. Well, one of the turkeys flew up in that live oak tree yonder on the corner of the square, and six little boys skinned up the tree and scooted out on the limb where the turkey sat. The limb broke off, and down came all six of those kids. Well, five of 'em just bounced up and took off after the turkey again, but the sixth one hit the concrete sidewalk, kicked a couple times, and lay still. They took him off to the hospital and I got a telephone report he was dead on arrival. So I wired in the story to all the papers I was correspondent for, and to two wire services, saying the boy had been killed chasing a turkey.

"So then the next morning after the story had circulated all over the state I found out the boy hadn't even been admitted to the hospital. Wasn't even hurt much. They just smeared a little monkey blood on his head and sent him home. Well, I got a few hot phone calls from my editors on that story. One of 'em said, 'Martindale, how come you didn't check with the justice of the peace for an inquest verdict? He did hold an inquest, didn't he?' What that editor didn't know, I was the justice of the peace myself at that time, and it just hadn't occurred to me to hold an inquest."

This dual role often proved complicated and confusing to Martindale's editors when they would call him for details on cases in his justice court. Sometimes they would discover that Martindale the justice of the peace would refuse to talk to Martindale the newspaper correspondent. "My feeling was," said J. Henry, "that there was certain evidence a J.P. just ought not to reveal to a reporter."

Martindale moves spryly about Lockhart on an artificial leg, a handicap about which he is completely insensitive.

He often writes about the advantages and disadvantages of his wooden leg, and considers that among the masterpieces he has turned out for the Lockhart paper was an account of how a local blacksmith fixed a broken leg for him by merely installing a new U-bolt in it.

"When I was a kid I used to run around here on a peg leg," J. Henry says. "Well, a farmer out here in the country once came round to my father and complained that I'd been in his watermelon patch. Said he could see the print of my peg leg all over that field, and that I'd punched that peg through the best melons in the patch."

J. Henry pleaded innocent but wasn't exonerated of the charge for a full quarter of a century.

"Twenty-five years later," Martindale said, "a bunch of guys around town here confessed that they'd raided that melon patch when I was home asleep and used a hoe handle to make peg-leg prints."

Today J. Henry sits and watches over the county's money, waiting for someone to come along to talk with and digging just for his own amazement into the various interesting incidents that have occurred over the years there in the Caldwell County Courthouse. Such as the time the county judge padlocked all the bathrooms in the courthouse because the commodes were running the water bill up, and it took court action initiated by the county commissioners to get the locks off again; and then there was the time the county attorney traded a couple of pistol shots in the hall of the courthouse with some citizen he was miffed at, and the day the city marshal was shot by the sheriff and fell dead right there in the office where J. Henry now serves as county treasurer, though that was before his time.

It has occurred to J. Henry, as it may have to you, that he has collected enough material to write a book about the early days around Lockhart. But he has publicly promised never to write it, and J. Henry says he feels his constituents will hold him steadfastly to the promise.

Rivermen, now, have the reputation of being interesting talkers. Some are, too.

William Larrabee Wells was. He's dead now. He lived in a sheet-metal shack on the bank of the Trinity River in Houston County. There he fished and sold bait to other fishermen and made friends. Thousands of them, from all over the nation, though he seldom left his riverbank home. Even after he got sick and near to dying, he didn't want to leave. Finally some of the friends just loaded him up and took him to a hospital.

I've known a good many men who spent their lives on the river. On the Trinity, the Brazos, the Colorado, the Neches. In the main they were men up in years when I met them, and they are dying off, and their places remain empty. Oh, there are younger men who come along and live in the same spots, but these seem to be on the river for different reasons than the old ones. I don't know a young man who has gone to the river for the reason that William Wells went.

Wells and his wife were living in Chicago during the 1930s when the Depression was raging. He had been educated at Northwestern University. Had a promising position in Chicago. Was making a good living. He was in perfect health, energetic, full of ideas, loved to meet people. The sort of man that goes far, as the saying is.

Then one day he put his wife in the car and just left. Went to wandering. He never again accepted a job that required him to stay under a roof. And in 1937 he ended up as keeper of a toll bridge across the Trinity River on State Highway 7. He spent the rest of his life there.

Why? "Because I found happiness here, and contentment," he told me. And that's something he hadn't found in a crowded city.

The spot where Wells settled is known to river fishermen over many states as Lock and Dam on the Trinity. Just above the bridge that carries State 7 traffic over the river stand the remains of a lock and a dam built in an unsuccessful attempt many years ago to make the Trinity a navigable stream. The swift water below these old ruins makes a dandy fishing spot, especially after a rise. I've seen cars from five states parked below the bridge at Lock and Dam when the fish are biting, and people standing shoulder to shoulder along the banks.

A toll bridge once spanned the Trinity at this point, and Wells's wandering happened to take him over that bridge when the job of tollkeeper was open. Wells was a short, stocky individual with smooth, swarthy skin and strong hands and the smallest feet I've ever seen on a grown man. He was into his seventies when I used to see him on the river.

People called him "The Old Fisherman." He would get letters addressed just that way, without any other name, sent to nearby Crockett. Fishermen living hundreds of miles away would leave him postcards so he could let them know when a good fish run was beginning. He told me that he had more friends than ever he'd have had if he'd stayed in Chicago.

I thought that "Old Fisherman" didn't fit him so well. For one thing his speech was educated Midwestern and you don't expect to hear a man living on a Texas river talking like that. But he fit in.

"I've had a lot of good times here on this river," he'd say. "And some sad times, too. I lost my wife here, and I've had to help pull several bodies out of this river when people drowned. Overflows have run me out of my shack

[134]

twenty-two times. When the old bridge was here, I used to leave the house during an overflow and go camp on it. The highway was underwater so there wasn't any traffic on the bridge. In the mornings I used to get up, row over here to the house, tie my boat to a table leg, put on hip boots, and fry my bacon and eggs standing in two and a half feet of water. There've been some good times here."

There's another man there on the river now in William Wells's place. He's a friendly, accommodating fellow, but his chief interest is farming the river bottom. He rents boats and sells bait like Wells did, but he doesn't live on the bank and fry bacon standing in two and a half feet of water.

Now you find different kinds of rivermen. I think William Wells's interest in the river was akin to Thoreau's interest in Walden Pond, though Wells was highly social and studied people as well as nature.

Thoreau's name likely wouldn't mean a thing to J. C. Collins. He loved the river but to him it also meant economic security, which Wells wasn't interested in. Collins was on a different river, too. The Brazos. I used to see his tent under the U.S. 79 bridge west of Hearne. He also fished the Colorado and the San Gabriel and the Little, and rivers in Kansas and Oklahoma. He did other things, too, but not for very long.

"Any time I couldn't find work, I headed for the river," he'd say.

There on the Brazos, equipped with boat and motor and nets and lines and the various licenses it takes to operate these items commercially, he'd range up and down a three-mile stretch of the stream. And sometimes you'd see him in Hearne, delivering his fish to restaurants or meat markets or to people planning a fish fry.

He didn't talk about the peace and contentment of life on a river, though I know he felt it. Mostly he spoke of fishing, and how you made a living at it. And about the biggest catch he ever made—an eighty-nine-pound yellow cat he took off a trotline right in front of his camp.

"Now a yellow cat," he said when I got him going one afternoon, "generally's thought of as the best eatin' catfish in Texas, but the blue cat's by far the fightin'est. Now you take an old yellow cat, weighs maybe fifty pounds, you get him boated and he just lays there and breathes. Not much danger him bitin' you. His bottom jaw sticks out too far. But a blue cat, now, there's a different thing. You put your hand in his mouth, you may draw back a stump. And he'll jump out the boat, too."

Is it true, as I've heard, that a big blue cat can drown a man?

"You bet it is true," Collins said. "Danger is, if he gets hold of you and gets you outta the boat, he'll whip you every time. Take you straight to the bottom if you don't watch. Fact is, any fish weighing better'n thirty pounds is dangerous for a man to tangle with in deep water. Fish has his power in water, where he's at home, and where a man's a stranger.

"I've cleaned a many a old alligator gar out of the Brazos. Caught 'em weighing up to a-hundred-and-ninety pounds, the kind that'll knock the sides out of a boat if you don't kill 'em before you boat 'em. These city fishermen, you hear 'em say a gar's no good to eat. Why, man, tenderloin of gar's some of the world's best meat. I've sold plenty of it four bits a pound, and there's maybe forty pounds of tenderloin on a-hundred-and-seventy-five-pound gar."

Is it dangerous, living on the river?

"Not for a man knows what he's doin'. I've been caught in several fast rises and had to paddle across fast water full of floatin' logs, and got thrown out a couple times, too. Nothin' serious."

River fishermen don't ask for too much in the way of excitement. They just want the experience of floating downstream, or rolling a big cat off a trotline into the boat, or sitting on the bank eating a meal of fried catfish, hot-water corn bread, and black coffee.

Collins had left the river when I saw him last. The banks were getting too steep for him to climb. But he was still saying, with that peculiar look in his eye, "I figure there's some old yellow cat in that river right today that'll go a hundred pounds."

I've lost track of Collins. I wonder if he stayed away from the river long.

In times long past, the ferryboat operators were some of my state's most stalwart rivermen, and doubtless were mighty interesting fellows to talk to. They are gone now, along with the ferries, but they haven't been gone as long as most Texans think.

As late as 1960 I rode the old Sheffield Ferry on the Neches River. At that time a bridge was being built to replace it, and a few months later the old boat was retired. Fred Jenkins was the operator and he still lives on the riverbank there by the ferry crossing.

For more than a century Sheffield Ferry took people and horses and wagons and buggies and automobiles across the Neches, providing a connection between Spurger in Tyler County and Kirbyville in Jasper County. The boat itself was a creaky old character, full of leaks and waterlogged timbers. I remember Jenkins' chief concern in those last months was whether the boat would stay afloat until the bridge was finished.

Even the road that led out of Spurger the few miles

down to the river was an old character. It began as a black-top, turned quickly into a sandy road, and finally degen-erated into a one-lane, two-rut affair winding through the pines and underbrush. You'd come across cows standing in the middle of that road as if they hadn't moved for a week, and squirrels and other wildlife would lope across in front of you. And just when you began to think the road would play out and leave you stranded out in the bottom, there was the river and the almost frightening, steep approach down to the water's edge and the ferry landing.

The Neches isn't a wide stream, which was fortunate for Fred Jenkins because the power that drew that boat across the river was provided by Jenkins' strong back. The boat was forty feet long and fourteen wide, built chiefly out of heavy two-by-eight timbers. It was held on its brief cross-stream course by a cable. To propel the boat, Jenkins used a peculiar sort of tool the name of which even he didn't know. It looked a little like an oar, except it was two-by-four-sized on the end with a deep slot cut in the bottom. Jenkins would hook the slotted end of that stick on the cable, haul back with a mighty heave, and the boat would move a foot or two. Jenkins is a strong fellow. He once let me try the stick when there wasn't any cargo on the ferry except him and me and my car. Pretty soon he took the stick back, without comment.

Five days a week the ferry was free, but on Saturdays and Sundays Jenkins charged fifty cents per car, because a good many people came down that river road on week-ends to ride the ferry just for the experience.

Fred Jenkins' father John operated the ferry from 1917 to 1946, when his son took it over. The old boat has been in the news a few times over the years. Such as when a couple of bank robbers used it in 1959. They'd cleaned out the bank at Chester, up in north Tyler County, and ap-

parently figured the law wouldn't guess that bank robbers
would choose a getaway route that featured an antiquated
ferry. You imagine it must have been a nervous river crossing for those robbers—sitting there with a car full of loot
and watching Jenkins haul back on the cable stick and
inch the ferry along, when likely the law wasn't far back
up the road.

Jenkins' father once carried Clyde Barrow and Bonnie
Parker across the river when that notorious pair was on
the way east, to be shot shortly thereafter by lawmen in
Arcadia, Louisiana.

Jenkins was toiling across the river with a winch truck
aboard one morning and the truck rolled off the end of
the deck and sank in ten feet of water. "Driver forgot to
put 'er in gear," Jenkins said, and shrugged. Another day
a young fellow came rolling down the steep embankment
to the ferry, hit the deck of the boat, and just kept going
—right off the other end. "His car floated all the way out
to the middle of the river," Jenkins said. "Had plenty time
to get out."

Jenkins patched that old boat and kept it pumped out
and pampered, and she served till the bridge was finished.
It was called by local people the last inland ferry in Texas.
I'm certain it was at least the last man-powered ferry in
the state. There's a ferry now across Lake Corpus Christi,
and it too is cable-drawn. Not by man power, though.

In Starr County, down on the Rio Grande, there's an old
sweetheart of a ferry that takes traffic across the river from
the Mexican town of Camargo in Tamaulipas State to Rio
Grande City in Texas. An "international ferry." I've ridden
it and it's an experience. It's cable-drawn and powered by
a big gasoline engine sitting on the Texas side. A Mexican
deck hand takes your fare and chocks your car wheels and
when you reach the bank he folds two narrow hinged run-

ners off the deck onto the bank. You've got to steer carefully to keep from dropping off in the water. The deck hand keeps a shovel handy. He throws two or three shovels of sand around the runners to make your landing smoother. It's the last of the old style Texas ferries.

I don't suppose you could make much of a case in favor of preserving public memory of old ferries, but it astonishes me how quickly people forget such things. Less than two years after the Sheffield Ferry quit operating I went back to the site to see what had happened to the old boat. A remarkable change had come over the area. A bridge across a river often invites what is grandly referred to as "development." People from Beaumont and Port Arthur had come up and built vacation houses on the riverbank above the bridge, and on Saturdays and Sundays they water-ski at the spot where the ferry ran. A couple of stores and a service station had sprung up. The man at the service station didn't remember Fred Jenkins' name, and spoke of the ferry as if it had been discontinued long years before. Lordy, it hadn't been but eighteen months.

The cuts in the riverbank where cars slid down to hit the ferry are still there, of course. The cables are gone, and the boat too. I went up to Fred Jenkins' house. He wasn't home, but his wife pointed out some heavy lumber stacked out behind the house—the remains of Sheffield Ferry, dismantled and curing in the sun. There was some good timber in that old boat, Mrs. Jenkins said.

CHAPTER 8

"I was skipper of a schooner, the Neptune . . .
*loaded with fuel and ice she drawed sixteen foot of
water."*

—Paul Blankenship

Jack Hillhouse doesn't just talk to you. He rumbles at you.
His deep and mighty voice rolls and growls and booms,
and blends with the sound of the Gulf coming through San
Luis Pass not far from Jack's front door.

Hillhouse is a man of the sea. Not a seagoing man, now.
That's a different thing. Jack lives on the beach. A beach-
comber, if you want to call him that. He doesn't care.

But whatever you call him say it with respect, because
his manner demands it. And if that's not enough, there's
his size—three hundred seven pounds, and so far above six
feet I bet four out of the starters on your alma mater's
basketball team would look up at him.

I've got Jack Hillhouse down in my book as one of the
ten most interesting guys I ever met. Not just because he's
a big man and not because he lives on the beach. But because of the way he lives there, and his reasons for being
there, and his views on the rest of the world.

But then I'll admit I'm drawn to beach people. Not the
summer sun worshipers. I mean the people that live on the
beach always.

Maybe this is because I was reared an inlander and
was a grown man before I ever saw salt water. They say
that's the kind that does the most dreaming about the sea.

Back in the old home town I used to sail the Atlantic standing on the quarter-deck of a British frigate with Captain Hornblower, and I saw all the oceans of the world when I signed on that whaler with Ahab and went hunting old Moby Dick. That was in my barefoot days, when every house in town had a big seashell sitting on the Victrola and if you wanted to hear the sound of the ocean you put the shell to your ear and listened to the swish and watched the surf in your mind's eye.

It always puzzled me a little that you could get the same sound out of a peanut butter jar or a tin can or a length of galvanized pipe. And sure enough the seashell turned out to be a liar. The ocean doesn't sound like that.

But the shell was the only way we could reach salt water in those days. Except for the rare times one of our schoolmates was unbelievably lucky enough to get taken far, far away to the sea on vacation. Maybe to Galveston, or even Corpus Christi, four hundred miles or more from home. There he would get to swim in the Gulf, and when school began in September he would be allowed long lecture periods in class to tell how the waves came in high as a person's head and how a jellyfish stings. Even the teacher, who hadn't seen the sea either, would listen and exclaim. And the kid would get A in geography.

The others of us didn't imagine we'd ever get to see an ocean and we churned inside with jealousy and thought it was hate. In retaliation I would put out to sea with Ahab and stay ten years, and learn what a spinnaker and a belaying pin were, and make friends with some giant of a man that would share his grog with me and who actually killed, barehanded, the ugly patch-eyed sailor that attacked me one night during the late watch.

It was thirty years after I created that friendly giant that I lay on the spare bunk in Jack Hillhouse's trailer at San

Luis Pass and listened to Jack talk about life on the beach. I thought about my old friendly giant. Hillhouse fits the mold perfectly and even after all those years it was a satisfaction to find him. Like most bony guys that never were very good in a fight, I like to be friends with a big man. There's a certain comfort and security in it. I suppose a psychologist would make something of that.

Hillhouse can stand at the door of his house trailer, look across San Luis Pass, and see the buildings of Galveston, twenty-five miles away. The view affords him no pleasure. He doesn't like cities, nor even small towns. So he lives in that little house trailer with a slick-haired dog named Greedy. The trailer is parked at the tip of Velasco Peninsula on a lonely beach. Jack has lived there, or somewhere near there, since World War II was over, and the sea seems to have accepted him as one of its creatures. His thick hair holds close to his scalp, not in curls but in ripples, like beach sand near the water. His eyes are small and blue and almost hidden by heavy lids that hang low and furnish protection from sand and wind.

You call on him in summer and he'll be barefooted and have his trousers rolled up above his knees, and he'll receive you with the gracious cordiality of a Southern planter. Jack knows people figure him for a character and he doesn't care. Now and then he goes into town—to Freeport or Alvin on business—and he'll walk in the bank with no shoes and his britches rolled up and people stare and laugh at him. Let 'em laugh. Jack just laughs back.

"I've got my friends," he told me. "They come down here and hunt and fish with me, and they like me for what I am and not for what I have, and that's the kind of friends I want."

Jack had three years of college. You hear it in his speech

sometimes, when he wants you to. He takes a lick at writing now and then, but doesn't like what he produces, and tears it up.

The pattern of his life was drawn in the Battle of the Bulge when he was commanding one of General Patton's tanks. He had to come out of it one day under unpleasant circumstances and a German burp gun caught him and tore one of his arms off. So when he came home he took to the beach and isn't sure why. "Maybe I wanted to prove I could take care of myself," he said.

"A man can get along down here without any trouble," he rumbled at me. "All he needs is a shotgun and a fish-hook and a sack of salt. Well, he wouldn't really need the salt. You can dip a spoon in these spots where the sea water has dried up and get almost pure salt.

"Then you have your birds' eggs. A curlew egg is very similar to a guinea egg. And the marsh hen, now, she lays an egg almost exactly like a chicken. They're good if a man knows how to get them. The way to do that, you pick out a nesting spot and stomp all the eggs you can find. Then the next day any eggs that show up in those nests are bound to be fresh laid."

Every few years a hurricane comes roaring up out of the West Indies and blows Jack off the beach. It doesn't matter. Like all beach people he just picks up the pieces and builds back again.

One day Hillhouse was walking barefooted in a marsh and felt something pricking his heel. Felt like a thorn. He looked back and a rattlesnake had sunk its fangs into his heel and was hanging on. He scraped the thing off and stomped it and went on about his business. The poison got to bothering him, though, and he had to go in and lie down.

"It wasn't a very big snake," he said. "I laid around for

a couple days with my foot packed in ice. Didn't feel too tough."

Later he was popped by a monstrous rattler. Rattlesnakes thrive in the coastal lowlands, though it's popular for inlanders to think that these evil-tempered reptiles live only in arid country. Storm tides show you just how thick the rattlers are on the coast. The snakes sometimes slither inland in great numbers during a hurricane, and they have a practice of sneaking into the houses of people who have evacuated on account of the storm. It makes a nervous homecoming afterward.

The big rattler that bit Hillhouse weighed twenty-two pounds after Jack shot the thing's head off. On account of the size a hunting friend insisted that Jack go to a hospital. He went but didn't like it, spent one night, and got up and walked out the next morning. "I had some duck hunting to do," he said.

Jack has been on the beach pushing twenty years. He long ago proved he could get along by himself minus an arm. That isn't why he stays now. I know why he stays. I could feel it there, that day we stood on the pier he built out front of his trailer house. He stays because the beach is home, and that's where a man ought to be.

Someday, I'll bet, progress will run Jack Hillhouse off his beach. Plans are working now for a new highway and a great causeway that will span San Luis Pass and connect Galveston Island with Velasco Peninsula, and the highway will run close by Jack's spot there on the beach. And that means more and more broad-beamed women in shorts and sunglasses will come looking for pretty shells along Jack's beach, and bring with them yelling kids and knobby-kneed men tagging behind lugging the lunch basket, and Jack's not going to like that. My guess is it'll send him looking for another beach to live on. I hope he finds it.

It was Rick and Dewey Rickenbrode that told me how to find Jack Hillhouse.

The Rickenbrodes live at Surfside Beach, about half an hour's drive down the coast from Hillhouse's trailer. By the sometimes curious standards of this world, Surfside Beach is considered civilized as compared with the quiet and lonely environment in which Hillhouse thrives at San Luis Pass. All that means is that you find more people around.

The first time I went in the little beach establishment operated by the Rickenbrodes, I ended up wondering who had gone crazy—me or everybody else in sight.

Rick's Place is one of I suppose a thousand similar businesses you find on the beach of the Texas Gulf shore. Beans and fish bait and potato chips and sandwiches and refreshments are sold by the Rickenbrodes, and on that first afternoon I was sitting quietly at one of the tables battling my thirst, when Mrs. Rickenbrode came along, picked up the bottle in front of me, and poured its contents down the back of my shirt. That makes a man catch up his breath.

Well, I sat there for a while, feeling the cool wetness spread down my spine and seep past my belt line, and considered what to do. Perhaps half a dozen other customers were present, and they watched me in a dead-faced way, as if the incident wasn't really anything out of the ordinary but was at least worth watching until something better happened. Nobody said a word or made a sound, except Mrs. Rickenbrode, who laughed heartily.

When I came out of shock and began mopping up, Dewey Rickenbrode's husband Rick bestirred himself, dropped a slug in the jukebox, took a pair of drumsticks from behind the grocery counter, and began accompanying the jukebox singer by beating out a rhythm on the corner of my table. The number playing was "When My Baby Smiles at Me."

"I made that record with Ted Lewis back in 1920," Rick told me, and added a brief résumé of his life prior to his arrival in Texas.

"I went through Colgate, Cornell, Minnesota, Syracuse, and Michigan universities," he said, "but I never got a degree." He kept tapping with the drumsticks.

"Did you see my oar?" Dewey Rickenbrode was back at my ear. I ducked, but she was only talking to me this time, loudly, over the noise of the jukebox and her husband's drumming. She pointed to a long stick of wood hanging over the jukebox. "That oar came off Noah's ark."

At this point somebody came along and pinned a red flower on my lapel and wired a freight tag on my shirt front. The tag said I was to be shipped by water freight to Savannah, Georgia. But an argument ensued. Two or three of the customers maintained I should be shipped not to Savannah but to Portland, Oregon. The discussion was spirited and I almost decided the participants were serious. They weighed all the advantages and disadvantages of being shipped to Savannah against those of being shipped to Portland, and in the end Portland won and a man came and changed the destination on my shipping tag.

It wouldn't have surprised me much if I had been picked up and loaded, but then a small dark-complected fellow came in the door and everyone's attention turned to him. Mrs. Rickenbrode parked herself in front of the newcomer, shook a finger in his face, and censured him severely.

"You were supposed to ride a horse through the front door this afternoon," she said, "and you let me down."

The man snapped his fingers. He had forgotten to bring his horse. He apologized for the oversight and promised he would ride the horse through Rick's Place tomorrow afternoon without fail. He promised seriously, just the same as he might promise his wife that tomorrow he would bring a spool of black thread he had forgotten again.

"Are you an official of the beach?"

The question was spoken loudly and sternly, and it brought silence behind it. I was reminded for a foolish instant of the horse opera at that point in the plot when the fastest gun walks through the saloon doors and asks if there is a dirty rat present by the name of Smith.

"I said are you an official of the beach?"

A small woman dressed in blue denims stood in the middle of Rick's Place. Her eyes were flaming. Her hands on her hipbones, the way women do their hands when they get all tempered up. It took awhile to realize she was addressing me.

"I intend," the woman said to me, "to get something done about whoever is shooting at that dog. It may be that the dog needs killing, all right, but it's wrong to shoot at that dog while our children are playing with it. I know it's not right and you know it's not right. Well?"

The silence was thick now, after that speech. Everybody present looked at me. It was plain I was expected to take some official action on this matter. The woman was convinced I was an official of the beach. Maybe it was the flower in my buttonhole, or my shipping tag.

It was Rick himself that got me off the hook. He started talking about his past again, taking advantage, I supposed, of the silence to make himself heard.

"I used to play with a circus band," he said, "and travel around. Do you know that at one time the ticket sellers for the circus received no salaries? All they got was what they could knock down by shortchanging the customers."

Dewey had taken the irate woman aside and was apparently explaining, I hoped, that I wasn't really an official of the beach. Rick was telling how the circus ticket men would gyp the customers—how a man with a wife and four kids won't really stop to count the change out of a twenty-dollar bill when the band's blaring under the tent and the children are howling because the show's about to begin.

It was an interesting story and I wanted to hear all of it, but five or six other people were seated at my table now. One of them was named Lonzo Gomez, and a fellow seated alongside him was accusing Lonzo loudly of being three hours late for supper at home.

Señor Gomez then rose, cleared his throat, and announced:

"A Latin is never late, for there is always *mañana*."

Everybody in Rick's Place cheered.

The show was over. Most, though not all by any means, of the strangeness that had gone before was just a way Rick and Dewey Rickenbrode have of initiating a new customer. It was a shameless frame-up. I knew it when the show was going on, because it all couldn't have been real, but still it was happening and it was eerie.

I went back to Rick and Dewey's many times after that. We came to be good friends and I got to know them as intelligent people with courage and a remarkable initiative and strength of spirit.

In 1961, when Hurricane Carla waltzed across Surfside Beach, wind and high tides picked up the little café of the Rickenbrodes and carried it away and they never saw it again. Only its concrete slab floor remained.

It was two months after the storm before I got down to the beach to check on Dewey and Rick. There they sat, on the same spot, already back in business. They had rebuilt their place mostly out of salvage they'd scrounged off the shore.

Rick was again on the job, tapping the table with his drumsticks and telling yarns out of his past, and Dewey was zipping about waiting on customers, talking about how glad she was that somebody far down the beach had found and returned her oar out of Noah's ark.

That old oar was one of the few personal possessions the storm left the Rickenbrodes.

"When I came back down here after the hurricane and looked at this place," Rick told me, "it was so ridiculous I just had to sit down and laugh. When the storm was going on, somebody called the Coast Guard boys down here about how things on the beach were standing up. They asked if anything had happened to Rick's Place. And the Coast Guard guy said, 'It passed here about three hours ago, goin' south.'"

Driving up and down the coast after that hurricane, I gained a tall respect for the spirit of beach people. They are the world's greatest rebuilders. When a storm wipes them out, they seem to take it as a personal affront, and they vow to build back and just dare another hurricane to hit them again.

Dewey Rickenbrode, though it seems out of character with her demeanor around the café, is a person with an appreciation of fine and delicate things. She had a houseful of antique furniture there on the beach. She had a shell collection she'd been offered two thousand dollars for. All of it went with the wind—to be seen never more.

"That storm taught me something," she told me one day when I caught her in a serious mood. "It taught me not to covet. I had some things in my house I truly coveted. Well, they're gone now, and I've learned my lesson."

Rick's summary statement after the storm was, "I'm gonna give it one more chance. But the next time I hear the word hurricane on the radio, I'm pullin' outta here and movin' to the Swiss Alps."

That's just talk, of course. If a hurricane blows their place away again, they'll build it back. They can't help it.

I like the beach best in winter.

People don't understand that sometimes, since the Gulf shore is, to them, so obviously a summer place. So they don't go to the beach in winter, and that's why they don't understand.

Take a city like Galveston, which is a summer city to most folks, and I'm happy they like to do their surfing and sun roasting there in the hot months, because that leaves it all to me in the winter. Give me a miserable, dark, and cold day to visit Galveston. That's when I like to poke along the beach where the sun worshipers frolic in summer. Everything is different in winter. Even the sea gulls behave differently. They sit around on the sea wall in quiet, ruffled groups and remind me of a bunch of old cows, waiting by the fence for somebody to come and feed them. The permanent people along the beach front take off their summer masks, and have time to talk to you, and be friendly. They make their money in summer, and do their living in winter.

It's tough to find genuineness on the beach in July. It's easier in January, when the beach people and the fishermen and the tugboat captains sit around in dim spots sipping suds and running their lives by again, enjoying the things that happened even more than the day they happened.

I wish I had done something I enjoyed talking about as much as Paul Blankenship loves telling about the time he skippered a millionaire's yacht thirty-seven miles out in the Gulf to Aransas Snapper Banks.

Blankenship is one of the tug captains. He lives nearly two hundred miles down-coast from Galveston. In Port

Aransas. In a narrow little house that somehow tries to look like a boat.

Port Aransas is the best town on the Texas shore to bum around in during winter.

It sits on the high end of Mustang Island, which spans the mouth of Corpus Christi Bay and gives protection to the tugs and barges that chug up and down the Intracoastal Canal. Port Aransas is a fishing town, chiefly, and fish are caught there the year round. But people fish chiefly in summer, and in winter there are many days when the blue northers reach down off the High Plains and make outdoors unpleasant all the way to the south tip of Texas. That's the time to hear the beach people talk.

Around eleven o'clock one cold and blustery night I was sitting in Aggie South's Grill there in Port Aransas, taking on one of Aggie's cheeseburgers, and this message reached me from the fellow sitting two stools down.

He was sitting a little hunched over, nursing a cool one, and he kept looking about with that open, receptive expression that a man puts on his face when he wants to talk. I guessed him at about sixty. Not the cap on his head or the dim light in Aggie's could hide the fact of his red hair. I couldn't see it, but he had the face that couldn't go with any other color.

Well, my business is listening to guys that want to talk, so I polished off Aggie's cheeseburger, moved to the unoccupied stool next to my neighbor and borrowed a light from him. He warmed up talking about the weather, about the depth of the Intracoastal Canal, about the population of Houston, and the damage done to Port Aransas by the most recent hurricane, and after that you couldn't have stopped him with a presidential order.

So by the time I bought him another cool one—an un-

spoken agreement understood by both parties in advance
—he had told me these things:

His name is Paul Blankenship. He is Irish and sixty-three. He skippers a tug, pushing fuel barges up and down the Intracoastal Canal. He has made a lot of money in his time, spent just as much, doesn't regret a cent of it, has had himself plenty of fun, and doesn't mind fighting a man.

"The biggest thing ever happened around Port Aransas," he said, "was when Franklin Roosevelt came down to fish."

So here came the story—the story of how it came to pass that Paul Blankenship got to shake hands with a president.

"I was snapper fishin' then," he said. "Commercial fishin', you know. That was in '36, maybe '37. I was skipper of a schooner, the *Neptune,* and she was a beautiful boat. Built in Corpus Christi. She carried six hundred yards of sail and a two-hundred-and-fifty-horse Superior Diesel, and loaded with fuel and ice she drawed sixteen foot of water.

"Well, we was hauled out for repairs at Corpus and I come home, here to Port Aransas. That was when Roosevelt was here. When he come he drawed millionaires to 'im like flies. There was twelve big yachts anchored here in the harbor and two destroyers out in the Gulf.

"Well, the first two, three days Roosevelt was here he didn't have much luck fishin'. So one of them millionaires asked me to pilot his yacht out to Aransas Banks to catch some red snapper for the President's party. I said I'd consider, and went on board the yacht. And I seen it wasn't properly equipped. So I told 'em I wouldn't go, because there wasn't no place this side of Galveston to buy what I needed. I needed some buoys and a grapplin' hook and a line to anchor that yacht in thirty-seven fathoms of water. Anyway I'd talked to that skipper and I could tell he wasn't no alligator (that is, didn't know his way around too well to be captain of a yacht). So I come on in and went to bed.

"Well, they come after me. Woke me up. I told 'em wasn't nothin' they could say to make me go without proper equipment, and outside of buyin' it in Galveston the only way would be go to Corpus and lease that gear off the *Neptune*.

"So that's what they done. They sent to Corpus with a truck and hauled that equipment back here and fitted it on the millionaire's yacht. Finally we left out of here about two o'clock one morning.

"Now Aransas Snapper Banks is thirty-seven miles out. That's nautical miles. And the true course from here is east southeast. I asked that yacht captain if his compass was true and he said it was. I thought, Well, there's one way to be sure, and I took a four-point bearing on Harbor Island Range Light. That compass proved out twenty degrees off. I allowed for that when runnin' my course, else I'd have met myself comin' back.

"Well, we got in that night about dark, and we must have had three thousand pounds of snapper aboard. They asked me to pick out some fish and deliver 'em to the President's yacht. I picked out two hundred snapper about eight pounds each, which I think is the best weight of snapper to eat. I delivered 'em and went aboard the President's yacht, and got to meet 'im.

"So that," said Paul Blankenship, reaching for his glass, "was the only time I ever shook hands with a president, or even seen one."

It was well past midnight when I left Aggie's, and Blankenship had promised to take me along sometime when he pushes a bargeload of oil up the Intracoastal Canal to Port Arthur. I doubt if I'll ever go, but I might. Meanwhile it's a comfort to know I could if I wanted to.

CHAPTER 9

*"I've been a thief all my life. Always had plenty of
money, and lived off the fat of the land."*
— Johnny M.

Almost a year of negotiation was required before Pat Craddock and I sat down together to record the story of how he
lost his left leg.

Not that Pat was reluctant to make known the facts of
this matter. It's just that he is a sensitive fellow in his own
way, and when he talks about the most important event of
his life he wants everything to be just right, to be in tune.
In this respect Pat's not so different from a concert pianist
who wouldn't perform on an instrument that's not tuned
up. Not so different, either, from a major-league pitcher that
takes his stretch and suddenly knows he's not going to
throw a good pitch, so he slips his foot off the rubber and
tosses over to first base. That way he gracefully avoids com-
mitting himself for the moment, and gets a chance to shake
off the uncertainty that besets him.

Pat Craddock had tossed over to first half a dozen times
during the year I stalked him, and then suddenly he sent
word for me to meet him early one morning and we would
have the story.

I waited for him outside a certain wire gap in a pasture
fence that skirts State Highway 6 in Grimes County. Off to
the east snakes the Navasota River, normally a muddy,
slick-surfaced stream when it sticks to its channel. The channel is too small. When the cloudbursts fall upstream in Rob-

ertson and Limestone counties, the lower Navasota slops out of its banks and spreads. Then its catfish, its gaspergou, and its cottonmouths swim forth from their channel home and wander along the sloughs and among the woods and brush that cover the river bottom. Oak, elm, native pecan, and a hundred species of low-growing bushy things.

Pat Craddock could name them all. His names would be different from those a naturalist would use. The naturalist might look at a small tree with oblong leaves and identify it as a member of the ebony family, *Diospyros virginiana.* And Pat would laugh and say, "Whatta you talkin' about, man? That's just a persimmon sprout."

Mornings, before town men leave the house for work, Pat comes up out of this tangled and often wet environment in his old car. He goes to the river long before dawn every morning to run his catfish lines. He also hauls stovewood (plenty of families in the Texas Post Oak Belt still eat hot biscuits baked in a wood-stove oven) and does some house and barn painting when he can get it. Pat's a scrambler. Got a family to feed.

He's in his middle forties. Lean and muscular. His face is long but it's open and friendly and grinning. It's a good face.

The sun wasn't long up when I heard Pat's old car groaning over the washouts as it climbed out of the bottom to the highway. It stopped at the fence and Pat was out and had the wire gap down before I could get to it. He moves around real spry on his crutches.

"I was workin' for this fella, cookin' whiskey up near Carlos when it happened," Pat told me, beginning at last the story of the missing leg. "A lot of whiskey was being cooked in Grimes County then.

"It was in April. April the twelfth, in the morning, when it happened. That morning early I'd already made one trip in to the still. Carried in a sack of sugar. Then I'd come out and was takin' another sack in. Well, the boss man had been tellin' me to be careful, and sometimes he'd slip up on me and give me a scare, you know, to see if I was being careful.

"I heard somebody comin' in on me that morning, but I thought it was just the boss testin' me again, and I didn't pay it no attention."

A bad error. It wasn't the boss. It was the law, making a raid on the still.

"When I saw it was the law," Pat went on, grinning as if he was telling of some practical joke, "I lit out of there. Later they said they called on me to halt. Maybe they did. I don't remember hearin' it.

"Anyway, the first shot they fired sprinkled me good, in the arms and back and both legs. I still got thirty-eight Number Four shot in this right leg. I tell my kids the leg's hollow and if they listen they can hear them shot rattle around in there.

"That first shot sort of deadened me all over. My legs felt like they wanted to fold, you know. I was already fallin' when they fired the second shot and that gave me a full load in the calf of the left leg. That one really curled me up.

"Well, they tried to make me tell where the whiskey was. But old stubborn Pat, I said I didn't know nothin' about any whiskey. It was hid good, and they never did find it. They looked around there for about two hours.

"I was beginnin' to hurt some. Bleedin' and all. I was shot about nine o'clock in the morning. Finally they took me to the jail at Anderson, and then over to the hospital in Navasota, which it was about 1 P.M. before I got to the hospital."

A couple of days later, Pat said, he was taken into Houston with gangrene in the left leg. It was amputated, high above the knee.

"I laid in that hospital in Houston seventy-eight days," Pat said. "And the first fifty of them days I hubbed plenty of hell. Finally when they turned me loose I walked out of there on these old crutches and hitchhiked home."

Well, that's about all there is to the story, and you may say it isn't much of a story to wait a year to hear. To me, though, it's a wonderful story. Not because it's about a man that violated the law but because of the honesty and openness with which it is told.

I'm not sure you'll understand that. What I mean is, Pat doesn't tell the story for any high and mighty reason. He doesn't tell it to gain sympathy or to show that he was mistreated by the law. He was cooking whiskey because that was his job. The law shot a moonshiner because that was the law's job. It's just the way things are.

He doesn't even tell the story to demonstrate that crime doesn't pay. Because in the first place Pat made a living at cooking whiskey for a good long while and therefore he knows it does pay sometimes. And if you think not, go and ask J. Edgar Hoover or even the constable in your precinct and they'll tell you it's true.

Still, I think it's important to Pat that his story be told and heard. Why? I can only guess. Pat wouldn't use these words, but I think he would agree that they express his reason:

"This is a thing that happened to me, and perhaps it ought to be set down on the record of human experience."

I often seek out people who have had their brushes with the law and listen to their stories. I'm not always certain, of course, that they stick to facts, but I like to listen to them because, like Pat Craddock, they deal in plain talk and a refreshing straightforwardness that "honest and upstanding citizens" so often avoid.

Sometimes I go to the state penitentiary to hear such talk. I'd a lot rather spend an hour listening to a guy that's doing ten to twenty for armed robbery than to the average banker or lawyer expounding on honesty or justice.

I think of Johnny M.

And I'm not certain why I hesitate to use Johnny's full name. Pat Craddock, now, just doesn't care, and would likely be insulted if his story showed up somewhere being told by a fellow with a fictitious name.

At the time I talked to him, Johnny M. didn't care either. But it might be that Johnny is in need of a break just now, wherever he is, and so I'll not risk spoiling any chance he might have to go straight. It's going to be tough enough for him the rest of his life.

But the day I talked with him, Johnny was a happy man. Two days earlier he had taken top money in saddle-bronc, bareback, and Brahman-bull riding in one of the roughest rodeos in Texas. He was in a good humor.

So he spoke congenially about his experiences at stealing things, like diamond rings, wrist watches, money, "stuff like that."

"I've been a thief all my life," Johnny said. "Always had plenty of money, and lived off the fat of the land."

I class that as one of the most remarkable quotes I ever heard come out of a man. It was delivered in the same tone and manner that an old pro baseball player uses at the banquet honoring him upon his retirement. When he says, as they all do, "Baseball has been good to me."

Now I don't mean to eulogize a man because he's a professional thief. So let it be clear to mammas and papas and scoutmasters that when Johnny made that statement he was sitting inside the high, red brick walls of the Texas

Department of Corrections. Which is just a bureaucratic way of saying the state penitentiary.

Johnny has been in and out of state prison several times. He had just come back in on account of stealing some saddles. He was glad to be back, and that's the truth, because he had returned just in time to qualify as a performer in the Texas Prison Rodeo. Johnny's an extremely capable cowboy.

It is Texas state prison legend that any number of former inmates of the system make it a point to slip off the straight and narrow in late summer so they'll be back behind the walls in time to ride in the rodeo. This famous show is held on every Sunday of October, the one month when an old prison rodeo rider had rather be in the penitentiary than out in the free world.

Some of Johnny's friends had told me he is one of the men that pulled a caper in order to re-enter prison for the rodeo. That's why I went to see him. To see if it was true.

Johnny said it wasn't, but added if that's what his friends wanted to think it was all right with him.

We talked in the rodeo office, behind the walls. Johnny had on his prison whites, the shirt open at the front to reveal a tattoo of Mickey Mouse on his chest. He wore boots and a yellow Western straw, pulled down in front so its sweatband almost touched his eyebrows. He's small, but a wiry fellow, and hard.

He told me about the events that led him back to prison for the fourth time.

"My stealin'," he said, "has always been out of safes, and jewelry stores, you know. This time I decided to get me some saddles. I've never fooled with cowboy stuff and I didn't figure the dope fiends and the jitterbugs would be stealin' saddles.

"But when they picked me up there must have been

twenty sheriffs come in to that courthouse to put a holt on me for stealin' saddles in their county. Why, it just seemed like *everybody* was stealin' saddles."

Johnny had some kind words to say on behalf of the district attorney that made a deal with him for a two-year stretch in return for a plea of guilty. A good swap, Johnny figured. He is a four-time loser and could have gotten a lot more time than that.

When a man gets a wide reputation as a thief, he is very popular among sheriffs in Texas. Johnny talked some about that.

"When I was in the free world this last time, I took my wife and my stepson to Oklahoma, just visitin'. I got a lot of friends in Oklahoma. Used to do some bootleggin' up there.

"Well, about every county we stopped in between Houston and the Red River, the sheriff'd try to put a holt on me for somethin' that'd got stolen.

"Like we stopped in Bonham, and stayed eight days. Now there hadn't been a burglary in that county in two years. Not a thing stolen. Not even a damn chicken. Well, in the eight days I was in town there was twenty-one burglaries. And when I left, the burglaries stopped."

The sheriff at Bonham, as you might expect, put a "holt" on Johnny. Their conversation went like this:

"Look at it my way, Johnny," the sheriff said. "Just suppose you're sheriff of this county, and I'm a professional thief. And I come into your county and stay eight days and twenty-one burglaries take place. And then they stop cold when I leave town. What would you do?"

"Why," said Johnny, seeing the point, "I just believe I'd arrest you, Sheriff."

Johnny told me he figured somebody who knew his reputation took advantage of his visit to Bonham and pulled the burglaries, figuring, rightly, that Johnny would get the blame.

"I never had nothin' to do with any of those things. And I ain't gonna lie about it. Sure, I may go out and get in trouble but when they catch me I'm gonna tell 'em just how it was."

Johnny takes pride that he has a reputation among peace officers for never telling lies about his stealing.

He said he really meant to quit stealing the last time he was out of prison. He was out on parole at the time. But he felt his parole officer wasn't doing right by him, and one night he went to see the parole officer, and they talked, and Johnny got all upset and hit the parole officer in the mouth. That's when he started stealing saddles.

The next time he's out, Johnny told me, he intends to do some rodeoing way up north "where there won't be a bunch of sheriffs tryin' to put a holt on me."

As a general thing, county jails in rural Texas towns are like public libraries in that they are slow to be replaced by new structures.

For this reason many Texas jails are now approaching antique status. The Milam County Jail at Cameron, for example. I have admired that old jail for years because it is such a character. Dark and red and rusty and experienced. It has a cupola on top where sparrows and pigeons live.

One day I got permission from the Milam County sheriff to visit the jail, and a constable walked me across the street from the courthouse to let me in. The jail occupies a lot that in a bigger town would be a choice piece of commercial real estate. It's on the town square. The prisoners can stand at the high jail windows on the second floor and watch the life and times of the county seat revolve around the court-house across the street.

I go in county jails now and then for the same reason I visit the state prison. To hear the inmates talk.

The constable unlocked the front door, put a key into a second door leading to the cells, and paused. "Have you got anything on you?" he asked. "I mean a weapon. Like a pocketknife? I don't say the prisoners would take it off you, but I wouldn't guarantee it."

I didn't have a pocketknife. The constable opened the door and I stepped through. He locked up behind me and said through the peephole, "I'll be back in an hour or so. You'll be all right."

He walked away and things became mighty quiet. I was in a stair well. Winding iron steps led up to the next level. The sound of voices above now came down the well, so I climbed the stairs, wondering how a prisoner locked up in a cell could take a pocketknife off me.

But the prisoners weren't locked in cells. The cell doors were all open and several men were out in the second level runaround. Three were on the concrete floor playing match-stick poker. Four others were sitting or standing around at the head of the stairway, just grinning at me, not saying anything.

Finally I said I was just visiting.

A tattooed fellow in the poker game laughed but didn't look up from his cards. "Yeah, that's what I said when they put me in here. That was two months ago."

From over behind the poker game a gray-bearded old fellow called out, "Say, how's the Kennedy Administration doing?" President Kennedy had been in office just a few months.

I told briefly what I could think of to say about the administration, including a report on the back trouble the

President was having at that time. All the prisoners listened intently.

A blond short-haired man about fifty stepped out. "You want to see some back trouble?" He walked to me, turned around, pulled his pants down, and exhibited a long deep scar on his lower spine. "Now there's some back trouble, Buddy. You got anything to smoke?" He adjusted his pants.

I handed out cigarettes and everybody became cordial. Scarback introduced the prisoners, not calling names but telling what each was in for. Some for being drunk. Some on hot checks. Some for stealing. The usual things.

"Now that guy there," Scarback said, indicating one of the poker players, "is in here for stealin' a pig."

"Stealin' a pig!" shouted a handsome curly-haired youth. He looked mighty young. He'd just been jailed the night before and hadn't heard about the pig. It struck him funny.

"Stealin' a pig!" he kept repeating between his laughing spells. "I believe I could steal somethin' better'n a pig."

Then the youth started talking about his case. His name was Mike and this was just the second jail he'd ever been in during all his long life. Said he was fifteen. Just the other day he'd gone down to Laredo with another guy, and they'd crossed the Rio Grande over into Mexico to Nuevo Laredo. Well, the other guy decided to stay in Nuevo Laredo awhile and he let Mike take his car to go see a girl.

The girl lived in Denison—up on the Red River, five hundred miles from Laredo. Mike tried to drive it without stopping. He went to sleep at the wheel in Milam County, ran the car in a ditch. The sheriff jailed him because the car had been reported stolen. Mike was confident he'd get out as soon as he wrote a letter and summoned help.

Mike and Scarback squired me around the jail, pointing out the views from various windows, talking about the food, describing their cases in detail. Men in jail often relish having an ear to bend. Even if they know the listener can't help them, they like to talk.

Mike asked me to come see the art work on the jail walls. It was good. Nobody knew who did it. Curiously the theme of this unknown county-jail muralist, working in soft pencil on a plaster wall, involved motherhood, patriotism, justice, brotherly love. It's not unusual to find this theme in amateur art on jail walls.

Well, I listened to all the troubles of Scarback and Mike and a few of the others, and by the time the constable returned to spring me, we were all friends. Searching for more smokes in my pockets, I pulled out my car keys and there on the key ring was a little silver knife I had gotten for Christmas. Not much of a weapon, but a knife all the same. I showed it to Mike and Scarback and told them what the constable said about taking weapons into the jail. They both laughed.

By the time I left Mike had promised me that he was going to stay out of jails from now on—though I didn't ask him for any such promise—and I had promised Scarback to bring him a couple cans of Prince Albert and some cigarette papers if the constable would let me. He did.

Look, I'm not a citizen that goes around trying to reform people in county jail and state prison. I go to such places because I'm a sucker for a story.

I doubt that the boy Mike will really stay out of jails. And I'm afraid Johnny M. will have a tough time avoiding the "holt" of sheriffs.

As for Pat Craddock, after he told me how he lost his left leg, I said to him that I bet it really taught him to stop cooking whiskey, didn't it?

"Whatta you talkin' about, man?" Pat grinned. "They've caught me at it again since then."

[165]

CHAPTER 10

"The lightbread people have ruined our women."
—Uncle Charlie Jones

In his general store at Kenney, in Austin County, August Tiemann keeps two stoves burning all winter. One is a gas heater that sits just inside the front door, and the other is a wood stove located about midway between the front and rear entrances.

I doubt Tiemann planned it this way, but those stoves serve two distinct purposes. The gas stove in front is for the comfort of customers who come in and buy something —a pound of cheese or a link of sausage or a chamber pot or a pair of overalls—and then go on home to supper. The wood stove accommodates those who come just to hang around for two or three hours and visit.

Tiemann is perfectly able to replace that old wood stove with a modern one, but he doesn't do it for the same reason that hundreds of other old-style country storekeepers in Texas hang on to their wood stoves. Which is that their customers are accustomed to standing around toasting their behinds with the penetrating heat that post-oak wood produces. Besides, you can't spit into a gas heater.

I pass Tiemann's perhaps two dozen times a year, but seldom stop except in winter. At dusk of a winter day when a fresh norther's blown in, it's good to go in August's place and back up to the wood stove for half an hour or so with all the others who love to do the same.

Sometimes a newcomer will wrinkle up his nose and say, "I smell something burning." And Tiemann will answer. "It's nothing. It's just the cats scorching."

The gray cats congregate there under the wood stove and sleep the winter away. Sometimes after August has stoked the stove the fire gets so hot the cats will get their fur scorched, yet they lie there and sleep away in perfect contentment. I've reached under that stove and stroked them to find their coats so hot I couldn't leave my hand on their backs, but they never move. "A cat," August explains to newcomers for the ten thousandth time, "can take an awful lot of heat."

So can Tiemann's customers. The price of cordwood being what it is, August could save money by throwing out that wood stove, but there is not any other way to provide for the comfort of his clientele. And anyway it wouldn't seem right to have that big fat old coffeepot heating on top of a gas stove.

Some days the customers around the stove are talkative and noisy; other times they just stand there and peer out the front of the store and watch darkness come. Customers dribble in, one, two, and three at a time, by both the front and back doors. The Negroes most often use the back door and do their buying in installments. That is, they'll buy a half pound of cheese and a loaf of bread and pay up, then they look around awhile, pick up a can of beans, and pay for that. They may make five or six purchases, paying after each purchase instead of gathering everything up and paying for it all at once, supermarket style. I've seen this style of buying many times in country-type stores. They say the custom originated in the days when the grocery money of country people was mighty short, and their arithmetic not so good—two circumstances still existing in many rural areas of this state. So the buyers bought and paid for one thing at a time to be certain they didn't buy more than they had money to pay for. It saved the embarrassment of having to put part of what they bought back on the shelf.

Every now and then some cub reporter, sent foraging across the state by his editor in search of a Sunday feature, "discovers" a store like August Tiemann's and grinds out a wide-eyed yarn saying that here, if the reader can believe it, yet stands an old-style country store that sells everything from notebook paper to horse collars. My only criticism of such a story is that its tone indicates that no other such store exists, that this is the last example of Texas country stores. Perhaps there's the reason many city dwellers have the notion that general merchandise, country-type stores have all but disappeared.

The fact is that this state is still salt and peppered with them, and the country store remains firmly entrenched as the hub around which rural life in Texas revolves.

In the last twenty years a great many rural communities, big enough at least to rate a name sign on their outskirts from the Texas Highway Department, have been slowly dying. Country schools have closed and the remaining students been sent to town to the better facilities of the big consolidated school districts. Young people, as a rule, no longer stay on the farm because of the terrific expense involved in getting started farming. Some once bustling country communities have flat disappeared.

Often the last place to go, however, in a dying community is the country store, which sometimes survives even the country church.

Apart from the obvious reason—that people remaining in the area still have to buy food and clothes and garden seed—the country store survives because even a fading community must have a center, a heart. A store is indeed the only institution that enables many rural neighborhoods to maintain identity as integral communities. Country stores were always more than places to buy merchandise. They are social centers, gathering places, sometimes even banking institutions supplying farmers with seed, fertilizer, feed, flour, and coffee against next fall's crop. Country storekeepers in the main are fairly astute businessmen, good talkers, and givers of directions, competent local historians, active community leaders, and patient answerers of questions from weekend motorists who come in asking, "Do you still sell high button shoes?"

There are country storekeepers who have no firsthand knowledge of a vacation or a day off, and then there are others whose business is such that they just don't bother about it very much. At Cawthon, in south Brazos County, I have sat around and jawed for two solid hours with Carroll and Russell Roark without ever being interrupted by a customer coming in their old frame store. It's my idea of good entertainment to sit with the Roarks and hear them talk about the beautiful fights that used to come off with dependable regularity every Saturday night at the Black Cat Tavern, just down the road from their store, and about river fishing, and about buried treasure. Carroll Roark took me to Old South Spring one day, to see if we could find the treasure tree.

"This old spring," he said, as we stood on the bank of the creek it feeds, "used to furnish pure water for a lot of moonshiners. But there was a fella had a still here one time that was making whiskey legal. Had a license and all, and he made a lot of money. But he didn't trust banks."

So you know what's coming. The man is said to have buried all his cash somewhere in the neighborhood, and people have been digging after it for half a century.

"Now this whiskey maker carved a peculiar sign on a big tree right near here somewhere. A real fancy job of carving.

It showed a snake chasing a turtle up a tree, and the story is that somewhere around in these woods there's another tree with the same job of carving, except it shows the snake chasing the turtle down the tree instead of up, and that's where the treasure's supposed to be."

So, as men will who don't have important things to do, we spent hours clawing through the woods and brush around Old South Spring trying to locate the treasure tree, knowing we wouldn't find it but not caring, savoring the old tales of ghosts that some of the local residents believe still inhabit those woods, guarding treasure as ghosts do. Roark, a quarter of a century my senior, walked my legs off through those woods and finally pronounced that the trees must have been cut down, or struck by lightning.

Which has little to do with country stores except as an illustration of the sort of men that keep them—chiefly congenial fellows with things to talk about other than business and traffic and the cost of living.

I think of F. K. (Papa) Bucek and the time he sat in back of his store at Hallettsville, talking about rheumatism.

"When I was just a youngster my father suffered from rheumatism, and one day I went with him to Fayetteville to see a man who was supposed to have a cure for the disease. It turned out the fellow didn't have the cure, but he told my father if he'd get himself some bees and work with them and let them sting him once in a while, he'd not be bothered by rheumatism. And it was so, and that's how I got started keeping bees. When I rob my bees I don't wear any mask and I don't use a smoke pot and I get stung pretty often. And I'm still convinced that the sting of those bees puts something in the blood stream that keeps a man healthy."

Doctors sometimes grinned at Papa Bucek's theory, but

they didn't laugh at the excellent state of his health when he was past eighty.

Then I enjoy remembering John Wessels, who operates a country barbershop.

To find Wessels' place of business, you drive north out of Warrenton, in Fayette County, take the first dirt road west, and follow its dips and turns for a mile and three quarters. Where the road forks you go north again and up ahead then you can see Wessels' white farmhouse.

Like as not he'll be down in the pasture seeing after his cows, but you can walk to the back of his cow lot and hail him and he'll come cut your hair. In front of the barn is parking space for customers, and the spotless one-chair barbershop is behind the white picket fence alongside his house. The shop has a linoleum floor and the walls are decorated with deer antlers, which Wessels' neighbors bring in, to make a sort of community hunting display. Prices are posted there among the deer antlers:

> Hair cut 50 cents
>
> Shave 20 cents

It hasn't been long since Wessels had to go up on the price of haircuts. You can see where he changed the sign. He used to cut hair for thirty-five cents. And yes, he is well aware of what prices are in city barbershops, but his customers are mainly his neighbors on surrounding farms, and he wouldn't think of charging them $1.75 for a haircut any more than they would charge him $1.75 for a dozen eggs.

Wessels' shop is never really closed. Most of his customers are busy during the day, so they come over at night. "I'd soon cut hair at night as just sit around the house," he says.

When the market on hogs and calves is down, or during drouthy weather when crops are short, Wessels has been known to come back down to thirty-five cents on haircuts, to help his customers out a little. As you can imagine, he stays pretty busy. Scores of young people off the farms in Fayette County have married and moved off to jobs in Houston, and many of these are inclined to let their children's hair grow till they get up for the weekend to visit grandparents. Then entire families troop over to get Wessels to barber them. Fifty-cent haircuts are just mighty hard to find in Houston.

Somehow it comforts me to know a man will run a country barbershop as more or less a community service. You find a few rural business establishments like that in Texas, though they're disappearing fast. Uncle Charlie Jones's store at Leggett, for example, in the pine hills of Polk County. The store is closed now because Uncle Charlie is gone. He kept that store not to make a living but as a place to meet his friends and talk about the days when he ran a saloon at Seven Oaks. And to boast with understandable pride about the four sets of children he and Mrs. Jones reared.

Uncle Charlie was a huge man, tremendously strong in his prime. But in his latter years his health was none too good, and there in the store he always sat in a straight chair nailed to a raised platform. This arrangement enabled him to get up and down easier.

It also gave him a sort of rostrum, or judge's bench, from which he delivered with sonorous oratory his opinions on world, national, and local matters. When he offered you a seat it would be an empty shell for soft-drink bottles, which left you sitting at Uncle Charlie's feet looking up at the oracle. My recollection includes a number of Uncle Charlie's pronouncements, but none sticks with me better than the opinion he delivered one day during a discussion of home cooking.

[172]

He said, "The lightbread people have ruined our women."

Now if you study that statement, you will see that it sums up a vast and complex situation in a mighty few simple words. If I can avoid ruining it by trying to explain it, on the surface the opinion holds that when the bakeries began turning out lightbread—a term once in wide use to indicate store-bought bread—then they planted what Uncle Charlie believed to be a deadly germ in American households. Meaning the women quit baking hot biscuits and corn bread, and from there went on to opening cans instead of shelling peas, and so on until they could play cards all day and rush home at five o'clock and thaw out something for supper. I am reminded by a certain authoritative source in my own household that there are those who would dispute that the American homemaker's role is so free of toil. I don't care to enter that argument. Still I class Uncle Charlie's dictum as a thing of beauty, enhanced by the manner in which it was delivered, as if the words were the only and final ones to be spoken in summation of a national question.

Uncle Charlie was the only man I ever met who once ran a saloon and who would talk about it openly.

"I went into that business sober," he would say from his raised platform there in the store, "and I came out the same way. I've always made a good many resolutions in my life and when I first put the key in the door of that saloon I promised myself I'd never correct a man's behavior while I was behind that bar.

"Now I wasn't in there barefooted [an old East Texas expression meaning he was prepared for trouble if it came]. I had me a good six-shooter and a Winchester and one of the best pair of brass knucks in East Texas. Let me show 'em to you." Then he'd raise with great effort out of his chair, hobble with his canes to the cash register, hit the no-sale key, and extract his "correctors"—the brass knucks. Then he'd sit down again, place the knucks and his right fist in the side pocket of his sweater, to illustrate how he approached a man who was trying to make trouble in his saloon.

"I'd walk out from behind that bar and put my left hand on the fellow's shoulder and I'd look him right in the eye, knowing these brass knucks would make two men out of Charlie T. Jones. Then I'd say, 'Now I'm Charlie Jones, and I'm your friend, so why don't you co-operate a little bit?' And the fellow would look at me awhile and then he'd generally say, 'Why, you *are* my friend, Charlie Jones, and I'll do whatever you say.'

"And do you know," Uncle Charlie would conclude, "I never had to hit a man in all my life."

A number of interesting citizens used to gather around Uncle Charlie's place. Now that he's not there on his platform any longer, I wonder where they go. Citizens like Walter Baxter.

Walter is a friendly-talking, slight-built sort of fellow of middle age. He seems a peaceable type, so that you are surprised to learn that he goes about armed at all times. When he would stroll slowly into Uncle Charlie's place about midmorning after making his accustomed rounds of the community, you could hear his ammunition rattling around in his pockets. The weapon he carries is the kind that country boys once used to shoot birds with, and snakes and lizards—made out of a pronged stock cut from a pine board or the small fork on a tree branch, two strips of inner-tube rubber, and a leather pocket trimmed from the tongue of an old shoe. It is no longer proper to use the correct name of this weapon in print.

Some now insist that the weapon should be called a sling-shot, which it is not. A slingshot is simpler and consists only of the pocket attached to a couple of long thin strips of leather. You put a rock in the pocket and whirl the strips of leather over your head and then let go of one of the strips, which sends the rock in the direction of the target. Or at least it will if you let go at the right time. It was a slingshot that the shepherd boy David used to conk Goliath on the noggin, knocking him down so that David could then draw the giant's own sword and cut his head off. For this accomplishment my admiration for David has always been boundless, for I can testify that it is very, very difficult to become proficient at hitting a target with a slingshot. You can get more accuracy with Baxter's weapon. If I do say it myself, the time was when I was a passing fair shot with such a contrivance, and I must grin at the thought of avoiding use of the name. I've walked a great many miles over mesquite and shin-oak hills, hunting with the Negro boys I played with in my growing days, and they too carried these weapons and called them by the correct name, and if an adult had told us we shouldn't use such a term (which none did), we all would have wondered why.

Anyway, what Walter Baxter shoots with his weapon is dogs.

As Walter himself explains why, several years ago Leggett got to be overcrowded with dogs lying around town, sleeping on the streets, and getting in people's way. So Walter, seeing the opportunity to be of public service, appointed himself to the job of teaching these dogs to stay home, where they're supposed to be. He patrols the streets faithfully and is an excellent marksman, especially on moving targets. When you pass through Leggett you may be able to spot Walter replenishing his ammo supply from the gravel streets and keeping an eye peeled for a dog with no business being in town.

One morning Walter and I went out back of Uncle

Charlie's store and he let me try out his weapon, and it was plain I had lost my touch, being unable to hit a quart vinegar bottle in Uncle Charlie's trash heap at a distance of twelve paces. Walter is death itself on such targets and is particularly adept at putting the blast on tin cans while walking along. This is the way he keeps his hand in—strolling along and suddenly throwing up and letting fly at tin cans. The fast draw. "It's getting so," Walter told me, "that when I see a dog all I have to do is throw up and the dog takes off for home. A lot of people around here have thanked me for keeping their dogs home. But a few tell me they don't want me shooting at their dog. But I tell 'em, we don't always get what we want, do we?"

That struck me as a pretty cocky answer for a little guy like Walter Baxter to be giving. But then I suppose he can back it up, being armed and all.

Uncle Charlie's was one of three types of country stores still to be found in Texas. These are wide and ill-defined categories and they are of my own making. Uncle Charlie's place was there chiefly as a place for him to meet his friends. The Roark brothers keep a store for a similar reason —not so much to make a living, but mostly so they'll have something to do when they are not on the Brazos River fishing. This is obvious, because they'll not hesitate to close the place up and take off for the river any day of the week.

August Tiemann's, and most other country-type stores I know of, is different in that it just can't close up without a stern and valid reason. That would be a handicap to the community it serves. Such stores in many communities are now building instead of going downhill, due to the fact that the city people are coming back to the country in their station wagons and air-conditioned pickup trucks, and bringing back to the country storekeeper at least some of the business he lost when the young folks all left the farm and went to town.

A third type of country store is the only kind that's actually called a country store by the owner. These have sprung up in the last decade on the main highways, and they flourish because their owners know that city people like to come in country stores, thinking they've discovered something. They are not really country stores, but nonetheless they are often interesting places, decorated with rusty horseshoes and plow points and wagon wheels and plastic steer horns—things that a genuine country storekeeper in business to serve a rural community wouldn't have around the place. August Tiemann, for example, has a counter where he serves customers refreshments. The seats on the stools lining this counter are old riding cultivator seats, but they are there strictly for purposes of utility and not decoration or atmosphere. The atmosphere around a true country store produces itself. In the new country stores on the highways, the owner produces the atmosphere by design.

Near Alvin, on State Highway 35 in Brazoria County, J. B. Choate operates a place that is one of dozens in Texas called The Country Store. A lot of people come in this store. Some come to buy, sell, or trade, and others come to sit in J.B.'s refreshment parlor, drench their thirst, and wait for J.B. to do something entertaining. If things get slow during the day, J.B. is apt to put on a straw hat, grab a secondhand guitar out of his remarkably variegated stock of merchandise, drop to one knee, and break out in spirited song. He seems to hold the guitar in such a way as to display the price tag—one such guitar he sold in this way for eight dollars and it didn't have but two strings on it—for J.B. is working at all times even when he seems to be playing.

Then he often says things that people enjoy. He will walk around the refreshment parlor sprinkling poison powders to kill flies, explaining that he does this only for the comfort of his customers. And adding, "I don't really have anything against flies as a general class. They don't eat much."

Now and then you'll see a group of people watching J.B. perform some chore, like taking the skin off a seven-foot rattlesnake to be nailed to the wall to enhance the décor.

Beyond all reasonable doubt Choate has proved the old saw which holds that if you put merchandise in a pretty package, the public will buy it no matter what it is. At one time, Choate offered his customers packaged buffalo chips, all done up in cellophane. He argued that this was a revealing commentary on human nature—the commentary being that the buffalo chips sold readily at ten cents per package.

Now why in the name of creation anybody would want a package of buffalo chips I don't know, and I suspect that J.B. didn't either. He sold them with calm detachment, never questioning the buyer's motives, maintaining the strictly fiscal attitude that if people wanted buffalo chips, then he'd give them buffalo chips.

As a source of this merchandise, J.B. naturally needed a buffalo. He got one, by the name of Joe, and J.B. kept him tethered out front of his establishment for several years. Joe was an even-tempered if untidy beast, and he openly cultivated the friendship of J.B.'s customers in the hope they'd buy him a beer. It was remarkable how many people would buy Joe a beer just to see him guzzle it down, with all the customary gulping and belching.

I would be hesitant to accuse J.B. of teaching Joe this stunt in order to increase his business volume, but at the same time I wouldn't want to insult him by suggesting he hadn't thought of it.

One of J.B.'s very regular refreshment-parlor customers

[178]

took a strong liking to Joe, and when he'd come in he'd buy two bottles of beer, drink one, and feed the other to Joe. This very fellow set out one day to determine Joe's capacity, and witnesses said Joe downed nine beers hand running. It was an inconclusive test, however, as nine was by no means Joe's capacity. The customer just got tired buying for two, remarking that Joe was nothing but a lush.

I disagree. I saw Joe one day when he was said to have seven rounds in him, and he was behaving like a perfect gentleman. I've seen men behaving worse after having had fewer.

CHAPTER 11

"Worryation is like sittin' in a rockin' chair. You goes back and fo'th, back and fo'th, but you never gets anywhere."

—Virge Whitfield

Virge Whitfield is a Negro farmer who lives "just by the scratch" on a deep sandy-land farm in north Burleson County. There he raises lady peas and other vegetables in his garden and supports two sisters and their "three head of children" and only heaven knows how many dogs. He also delivers, to most anybody that comes along, a series of pearly wisdoms and Scripture quotes and parables, about life and love and courage and proper conduct.

When you go to Virge's place, you take somebody with you that knows the way. He lives about six wire gaps beyond pavement. The road switches course from year to year. You'd need to ask directions if you went alone, and a stranger stopping at Negro farmhouses asking where So-and-so lives sometimes gets a mighty little co-operation, at least until he makes clear just why he wants to locate his party.

The friend that last took me to call on Virge handed him a gift of two United States dollars when we had honked him out of his patched-up house and to the front gate. Virge walked slow and shuffly, for he is nearing eighty and is stooped and stiff-legged from long years of labor. His eyes lighted up and his face turned to a grin a yard wide when he saw the two dollars.

"Lawd, Lawd," he sang out, throwing his arms up and viewing the skies. "Trust in the Lawd, I say, and purty soon somebody'll come along that ain't tight."

Two dollars, plainly, amounts to a substantial subsidy for Virge. Getting along just by the scratch, as he says, means he doesn't see much currency. As if the money were a fee for which he expected to perform, Virge immediately drew out of his old trousers a pocket watch, one of his great treasures. He keeps it wrapped in a thick cloth. He unwrapped that watch slowly, reverently. He spread the cloth on the hood of the car, placed the watch in the center, and viewed it a moment, as if it were a great gem.

"Now," he said, "I'm gonna tell you about this watch. A watch ain't just to tell time by, and it wasn't named a watch just so it would have a name."

Then he began a melodic, rhythmic chant. "Now, how you gonna spell watch. You spells it W-A-T-C-H. Now think on them letters. Whatcha wanna think on W for? Well, W stands for words. You wanna watch your words. You can speak words that make hate, or words that make love, so watch your words.

"Now I'm a'leavin' W and goin' to A. A stands for action. You wanna watch your action. And don't never judge another's. Supposin' a man walked buck nekkid in the streets. You gonna hate him for that, or will you love him anyways because he's a human bein'? You wanna watch your action.

"Leavin' A and goin' to T now. T is the tongue. You wanna watch your tongue. The Bible say a soft answer turneth away wrath, but grievous words stirreth up anger. So watch your tongue.

"Goin' to C. C is for character. Birds of a feather flock together, so watch the company you keeps.

"Goin' to H now. H is the sweetest letter in the alphabet, because it stands for heaven, health, happiness, and home.

[181]

Folks may say it stands for house, but that ain't right. You can build a house but you can't build no home, because a home is in the hearts of mens and womens, and ain't made out of no planks."

Virge took up the watch again, wrapped it carefully, tucked it into his pocket. "I think of old Alexander the Great," he began again. "I always like to read about him. I didn't go no further than the sixth grade accoun' that's far as they taught, but I said I went to a high school because it was on a hill. I think about old Alexander when his father Philip bought a fine new horse. The horse's name was Cheroobus, and he was wild, and caperin', and nobody was brave enough to ride him because they was afraid they'd be destroyed. But Alexander came up and he says, 'I'll ride that horse,' and he turned the horse's head into the setting sun and crawled on him and rode off and the people looked after him to be destroyed. But he wasn't, because he seen that horse was only afraid of its shadow, and wasn't wild when he was turned into the sun."

From this lesson on courage and its relationship to intelligence, Virge moved on to a parable illustrating that bouquets are due the living, not the dead.

"There was a woman took low sick, and near to dyin', and her friend stayed by her side long days and nights, seein' after her. So then she died, and the people were afixin' for her funeral, and they had beautiful flowers coverin' her coffin. When the friend that's nursed the dead woman came and seen the flowers, she went away and brought a bowl of soup, and set it up on the coffin. Well, the people laughed at that, and thought they'd have a little fun, and they said, 'You think that dead person can eat that soup?' And the woman that brought it said, 'I think she can if she can smell them flowers.'"

Virge delivers these little speeches with elaborate gestures

[182]

and grand inflections. Sometimes he gazes out over the pasture, as if the post-oak thickets are the multitudes he is addressing.

And always surrounding him are fifteen to twenty of his dogs, scratching, grunting, snoring, wallowing in the sand at Virge's feet. Out in the thickets, around the barn, under the house, are many, many more dogs. You hear them, get glimpses of them. Nobody knows how many dogs Virge keeps. Not even Virge. Possibly a hundred. Maybe even twice that many.

Now, maybe you remember when you were a youngster that you met an old dog on the road, and it didn't seem to have a home and it loved you immediately and followed you home. And maybe you remember how it made you feel when you weren't allowed to keep it. Near as I can figure, Virge Whitfield has maintained this view of dogs in general all his life, and since there is no one to tell him he can't keep a stray dog, he just keeps it. He hunts with the dogs some, but there is not a fine hunter in the lot. They're mostly just old cold-blooded dogs, lean and flop-eared and cowering and ugly.

I once heard a story, passed on from some of Virge's neighbors, that if you try to count his dogs he'll kill you. Some of his neighbors believe it, too. I don't. A softhearted old fellow like Virge wouldn't kill a man.

Yet it's a fact he'll resist having the dogs counted. A friend of mine who once farmed near Virge's place began counting them one day. Virge fell to his knees and pleaded with the man to stop counting. My friend thinks it's because Virge considers it bad luck to count the dogs. Or, more likely, that he'll discover some of them have died or have run away, and that would make him sad.

This very day, if you went to Virge and told him of an old dog that lay sick and hungry and homeless, Virge would go get it and bring it home. People whose words I consider solid say they've known Virge to walk as far as twenty miles to pick up a sick dog and walk home again carrying it. He'd have to walk. Doesn't even own a mule. People often see him in the post oak carrying wood, on his back, to cook with.

The man that tried to count Virge's dogs once said to him, "Virge, since you're so good with dogs, we ought to go into the purebred dog business. We could raise some good dogs and sell them. I'll get the dogs and stand the expense of feeding them and you can care for them and we'll split the profits. But of course you'll have to get rid of these old soup hounds around here, else we couldn't keep our dogs purebred."

Virge refused the proposition, much as he needed the money. He wouldn't part with any dogs, even to get more. Anyway he's opposed to selling a dog. Doesn't think it's right.

He insists that Scripture describes a dog as man's most faithful companion, though I can't find any such thought in my Bible. "You do a kind thing for a horse or a cow or a hog and then turn him out in the pasture he'll forget it. Not a dog. A dog won't forget it."

Maybe it wouldn't, if Virge were dealing with it. He seems to have an almost supernatural understanding of dogs. He can handle with ease a vicious dog whose owner can't even touch it. Says he has never, ever been bitten. Some say it's only the good and kind who have such an understanding with dumb animals. I've known some exceptions, but Virge is no exception. I class him one of the truly good men that I've met.

His neighbors say that during the Depression of the 1930s Virge kept sixteen Negro families from starvation with the produce from his sandy garden. He's a master gardener. Plants by the signs of the zodiac, and his vegetables come up to perfect stands in beautiful geometrical designs.

I find something a bit sad in Virge Whitfield. It's not just that he has a tough time making a living for the people and the animals he loves. I think it's his faith in the goodness of human beings. I mean after seventy-eight years of living just by the scratch he yet holds out hope that someday everybody in the world will love one another and go about doing kindnesses for their fellow beings, and then everything will be all right. What's sad about that? Why, it's sad because so many of us, including myself, seem to have lost faith that people will ever love one another any more than they do now. I'm afraid Virge will go to his grave still a poor and kind and good and disappointed man.

During the visit on which my friend gave him the two dollars, Virge had a favor to ask. He'd heard that the friend's beagle bitch was about to have pups. He wanted one of them. A female, if he could get it.

The pup was promised, and we drove away. Virge shuffled back toward his front stoop, talking to himself, praising the Lord, thumbing the green bills, and invoking a blessing on people that ain't tight.

Virge Whitfield may live to be a hundred. It isn't very tough to find people along the Texas coast who make it past the century mark, especially among the rural Negroes. A lot of whites will tell you it's because the rural Negro doesn't know what worry is. I doubt that, but it's as good an explanation as any. I do know they are generally inured to hardship, and the discomfort that accompanies life past ninety they seem to accept as just another trial to be endured with the composure they endured countless others in past years.

An aged Negro is viewed with a certain curious respect

by white people in rural Texas. He is considered something special, somebody whose folksy philosophies are worth listening to, a person that's all right to go to see, and sit and visit with. It doesn't have anything to do with civil rights or integration. People are always saying to me, "Say, there's an old colored fellow, Shepard's his name, lives out at Stoneham. Fine old fellow. Like to take you out there. Hear what he has to say."

The result is I've spent many hours the past ten years sitting in the homes of Negroes out in the pine timber or the post oak, and smelled the familiar bitter odor of turnip greens cooking and the mustiness of wood-burning stoves. At such times the civil rights question and the race riots and the integration suits all seem remote and senseless. A white man doesn't know what gracious treatment is until he becomes the house guest of a Texas rural Negro.

One like John Shields. Shields didn't make it to his hundredth birthday, though he came close. It was three years after I talked with him at his little home in north Fayette County that I heard he'd died. He was ninety-four then. I'll not forget him because of the first words he spoke to me.

We were sitting on his front porch. "When I was six years old," he said, "I was given away. Just like you'd give away a cat or a chicken or a dog. Way it happened, my father married another woman. He had eight children then, and she had eight children and that was too many to feed. She used to put more food on her children's plates than she'd put on mine, and I'd tear into 'em. So finally she told my father that I had to go or she'd leave. Well, he gave me away. My father didn't want to lose that woman because he was proud of her. She was a yellow woman, and I was black. So he gave me to a German family and they raised me up among white folks. I had plenty to eat and they gave me a jack to ride, and later an old horse, and they taught me to read and write."

Shields slumped a bit in his porch chair. His white side-burns and mustache curled over his dark face. Even then, when he was past ninety, his arms and shoulders were heavy, still well muscled. White men once gathered to watch in wonder as John Shields, when he was a young man, wrestled five-hundred-pound bales of cotton off a loading platform onto a wagon, all by himself. He was a great favorite among children both black and white, and you still hear people speak of how he used to take a raft of children possum or coon hunting and come home carrying four or five of them on his strong back. It was a hot day when I visited Shields and he sat barefooted in the porch chair. A small yellow kitten lay curled around one of his feet.

Shields raised his head and looked out at the Triumph Baptist Church, which stands about a hundred yards from his front door. He was superintendent of that church's Sunday school for more than fifty years. A week earlier the church had honored him for his services, and Shields drank it all in and thought it was nothing but right.

"The Book says give honor to whom honor is due," he told me. Then he grinned a little. "Well, I've been with 'em in the church now for all those years, and I never paid even a five-cent fine, and I never been arrested by anybody, and if I ever stole anything nobody ever missed it, and even if they missed it they didn't know I had it."

Then came his deep slow laugh, like thunder in clouds beyond the horizon. In his last years Shields spent his time reading the Bible and watching television. Curiously, his favorite television personality was Dick Clark, the rock-and-roll record plugger. But Shields's mind had trouble adjusting to the fact of television.

His daughter who lived with him told me, "Papa thinks the people on that screen are alive. He speaks to Dick Clark, and to Cochise, and he thinks they speak back to him. He doesn't like the cowboys much. He tells me to turn 'em off, before he gets shot."

Shields frowned a bit at that. He gestured by flipping one ankle quickly, and the yellow kitten sleeping on his foot sailed about three yards off the porch and sprawled, surprised and sleepy-eyed, in the sand of the front yard.

He said, "My daughter says there ain't no life in that television. But they talk to you, and they sing to you, and they dance for you, so I say there's got to be life from somewhere."

Shields and I talked about the atomic bomb, to which he was opposed on religious principles. Said bombs didn't please the Lord. He thought shooting rockets at the moon was foolish and would make the Lord angry. He was certain the Russians had hit the moon with a rocket because he could see, when the moon was right, a new scar on that satellite where the missile struck.

When it was time for Dick Clark's program, I left. By then the yellow kitten had crept slowly back up the porch steps and curled itself around John Shields's bare foot again.

Robert Shepard's first wife died in 1908. His second died in 1926. As far as I know he is still around, pushing on toward a hundred.

When I sat in his house at Stoneham, in Grimes County, he was in his mid-nineties and one of the most astonishing physical specimens I've ever seen. White-haired, sure, but straight as a soldier. Just a tiny bit hard of hearing. He talked and got about with great energy and enthusiasm. He could read a newspaper from front to back without glasses.

He had a pair once but they bothered him so he threw 'em away.

"Forty years ago I had rheumatism," he said. "Had it so bad I had to lift my feet out of the bed every morning. But I cured it by taking soda. Rheumatism, you know, ain't nothin' but acid in the bones and the soda counteracts it. When I was eighty-eight was the first time I ever fooled with any of these doctors. I came down with the chicken pox. Well, I didn't pay no attention to it, and kept agoin', walkin' in the rain and all, and I got double pneumonia. They put me in the hospital for a little while.

"I can remember when Grant was president. I was a boy of ten workin' in a cotton patch at Roan's Prairie when Grant left office, and when I was twenty-nine I cast my first vote for a president. I voted for McKinley. I had two brothers born into slavery at Roan's Prairie, and I was born in 1867 just two years after the end of the Civil War.

"I saw a man hanged at Anderson once. They said he killed his wife for her policy. That was in 1895, I think it was. A piece out from Anderson they built a gallows. In those days a man rode to the gallows on top of his coffin. I recollect that fellow's last testimony. He said, 'When this rope tightens on my neck I know I'll meet my wife in heaven.' When he fell through the floor, two or three women fainted. It's a bad thing to see a man hanged."

It's an overworked question, but I naturally had to ask Shepard how he managed to stay healthy through so many years. He said it was partly his walking, that he walks a mile to his mailbox every morning, and partly that he keeps up with things—reads newspapers and books, interprets the news, analyzes politics from McKinley to Johnson. Works hard, too. He'd been cutting post-oak sprouts out of his watermelon land that spring day and said with a rain he'd be plowing in another week. He also laughs a lot and thinks it's important. He never lets the sun catch him in bed, gets up Sunday morning same as Monday.

Or if you insist on a formula, Shepard has that, too: "Trust in the Lord," he said, "and keep astirrin'."

The woods in East Texas are full of Negro preachers living long past the average life span. Preachers like the Rev. Jefferson Norris.

Two or three people had written me about Norris. White people who'd known him all their lives. One said he really felt that Norris had the gift of eternal youth. I wasn't certain the man meant that literally or figuratively, but it whetted my curiosity and one crisp fall day I drove up in Leon County to search Norris out.

He lives in a comfortable farmhouse with a tin roof and a long front porch trimmed in green. It stands way back in the post oak, behind a couple of wire gaps from the blacktop. I drove up in front and honked once and then stood at the front gate and called, because a couple of rangy, noisy dogs didn't seem real friendly.

Long ago I learned my lesson about going into fenced yards with strange dogs. I just don't do it any more, and when dogs come racing up to my car out in the country I stay put until somebody calls them off. I got myself in a fix one time walking into a fenced yard with dogs in it.

It was at a house about like Jefferson Norris's, with a chicken-wire fence around it and a sturdy gate. Except there was a sign on the gate. "Beware Bad Dog," it read. I couldn't see a dog around, but I stood at the gate and called a time or two. Presently here came the dog. A little woolly dog about a foot long. He came wagging up to the gate and stuck his nose through and licked my hand and made happy noises. Bad dog, indeed. But I know some people will put up a beware-the-dog sign just to discourage peddlers and snoopers, even when they don't have even one dog around the place. So I opened the gate and went on up the path to the front door and stepped on the porch.

Of course there behind the vines on the porch was the dog that the sign referred to. And he was big and stiff-legged and high-tailed and yellow-toothed, and the noises he was making weren't friendly. He didn't bark. I know the old saw that says a barking dog won't bite isn't all truth, but give me a barking dog if I am inside a fence with him. When a dog doesn't bark I get the feeling he is saving up energy to chew on me.

I began to back off the porch slowly, convinced that the beast would be at my throat just any second. The little woolly dog was still at my feet, and now and then he'd raise up and put his paws on my leg and I'd pet him gently and say friendly things, figuring maybe that big growling animal on the porch would notice that I was kind to creatures of his species. I backed out to the gate and slipped through it quickly and thankfully. The big dog had come out on the path and he stood there with fire in his eye and his expression said, "Buddy, you better not come back." And I didn't, and that little incident taught me to respect beware-the-dog signs and never to go in fenced yards in the country until I can raise somebody out of the house.

At Jefferson Norris's front gate that day, a tall Negro man finally answered my call. He was in working clothes. Patched blue denims, a sweater under a brown coat, and a leather cap. He looked about forty. I'd been told Norris had a son, and I asked the tall man if Rev. Norris was home. The man said he was Rev. Norris.

I must have stood there and studied his face a long moment then, and I might have looked doubtful. Rev. Norris was supposed to be ninety years old. This man hadn't any more wrinkles in his face than a thirty-five-year-old.

His walk was straight and quick. His handshake was strong and his eyes clear.

"I'll be ninety next May thirteenth," he said, and grinned a little because he'd guessed the question I was thinking. He showed a row of white teeth tipped with gold. It wasn't difficult to see why a person might believe Norris had been gifted with eternal youth. This man was thirty years old before he ever became a preacher, yet he's been pastoring country churches in Leon County now for sixty years. We sat down in the warm sun and talked about it.

"I like to say I'm a self-made preacher, with the Lord's help," Norris said. "I never did do much schooling for it, but I had religious training from my early days. My father and my mother were both religious. My father was a deacon and he trained me and my brothers and I haven't used an ax to cut a stick of wood on Sunday since I don't know when.

"But other days I still work. Still chop wood. My fireplace and chimney there on the north end of the house, my son and I built that not long ago. I feel better stirrin' around than just sittin' around. Me and my boy we've got some cattle, and we raise a little truck, and some feed for the stock. I took to doing farm work when I was seven and you could say I'm still at it. I preach to my folks that an idle mind is the devil's workshop."

Maybe half a mile across Rev. Norris's pasture is his church, the Galilee-Living Hope Baptist. "Now it used to be two different churches, is why it's got a double name like that, and at that time I was pastorin' both of 'em. Well, it was a little jealousy there. Maybe one thought I was doin' more for the other, so I left and took a call to a church at Centerville. But in about two years they called me back here, and I said, 'I'll come if you'll unite these two churches.' So that's what we did."

When Norris said unite the two churches, he meant for

them to unite in more ways than one. The churches were a couple miles apart. He had each congregation tear down its frame building, haul the lumber to a neutral spot, and use the materials from both churches to erect another building.

The old pastor talked awhile about the economic condition of his people. "They's some in pretty good condition and some not. And some's left and gone to cities. The farm work's about played out and that's how so many of them made their livings. I don't know what most of 'em would do if the Lord didn't send help from the government."

I questioned Norris about that last statement, which some may consider to be a curious view of government relief. He is truly convinced that public welfare funds that help feed his people come from heaven, at least indirectly.

"On Sundays," he said, continuing the evaluation of his church community, "we won't have but about forty head in the congregation. Used to have seventy-five or eighty. Why, one Sunday after a revival I baptized fifty head in Paddock's Lake. We had a big crowd there, lot of white folks, all around that lake shore watching.

"The white folks here always treated me good. When I gets down on my knees to pray, I prays for the white folks the same as anybody else.

"My brother Jacob was two years older than me. He's gone in. We cleared this farm with axes and burnt the brush and paid for the land. But now all my brothers has gone in. Still I don't think about retiring. I just love to work for the Lord, and I don't believe it'd please Him if I quit. I read my Bible and I don't see where it gives me leave to retire, no matter how old I get. I think about old Hezekiah. He was gettin' ready to go in, you know, but he talked to the Lord and got fifteen years added on.

"It just seems like the Lord's got me reserved."

[193]

CHAPTER 12

"Knew a fella once that was troubled bad from sore eye. Had it for years. Well, one day he was runnin' traps and caught a skunk by mistake, and that skunk sprayed him good, right in the face. And do you know, he was never again troubled from sore eye."
—John Estes, wolf hunter

Long-distance telephone operators in little Texas towns have lately become just mighty sophisticated. This has happened only since modern dial phone systems have been installed to replace the old ones. Purely from a personal view, I am opposed to fancy phone setups in country towns because they're so impersonal.

A little after the new phones came to his town, I called a fellow who is known to every last person in the rice farming community he lives in. I have called him I guess a dozen times in the last decade and have never known his number because I didn't need it. I would just tell my operator his name and his town and if she asked for his number I would say the operator on the other end would know it. And she always did.

So I was puzzled to overhear the operator in his town asking how this party spells his name, and how he is listed in the directory, and a lot of other particulars that no operator in that town ever asked for before. Great Scott, that fellow's grandfather built the town, and his father ran it almost singlehandedly, just as his son does now, and anybody living there that doesn't know that name must surely have just been shipped in from Up East.

What a difference. Why, not two years ago calling that guy was a nice, newsy adventure. I would put in the call and sit back and listen, and the operator on his end would say to the operator on my end, "Lordy, Operator, I don't know if we can find him or not. Just a minute."

Then I could hear her questioning a co-worker there in the office. "Geraldine, got any idea where J.M. would be?"

A pause while Geraldine answers. Geraldine is J.M.'s niece. The operator, having consulted Geraldine, comes back on and says, "His niece says he just left to go to Houston. But we might catch him at the Highway Cafe. He stops out there for coffee sometimes. Just a minute."

So she rings up the Highway Cafe.

"Jimmy?" she says when the owner answers. "Is J.M. there? I've got a call for him."

"He just left here, May," Jimmy says. "You might catch him at Cole's. Said he was goin' by there to get a pickup reel. They're cuttin' his rice today on the Stewart place."

"I thought he was goin' to Houston to meet Ruth," May says.

"Naw, he had a letter from her this morning and she's not comin' in till Thursday."

"Did he say how Ruth's mother was?"

"Yeah, said she's gonna be all right. Still in the hospital, though."

"Listen, Jimmy, if he comes by there tell him to give me a call, will you?"

"Sure will, May."

So then May rings up Cole's place, a farm-implement house.

"Buddy?" says May. "Is J.M. there?"

"Haven't seen him, May. Not since six o'clock this morning. Just a minute. Maybe Jack knows."

Buddy turns from the phone. Jack is J.M.'s nephew.

"Jack says J.M.'s gone to Houston, May, to meet Ruth's plane."

"Naw," May says, "she's not comin' in till Thursday. He had a letter this morning. Jimmy said he just left the café to get a pickup reel at your place."

"Is Ruth's mother worse?"

"Don't think so. But she hasn't got out of the hospital yet."

"Hold on, May. Here's J.M. now, just driving up."

"Put him on, will you? I've got a call for him."

Now I ask you, should it be necessary to know the phone number of a guy like that to place a call to him in the town that he practically owns?

Whether May still works as an operator in that town since the new phone system was installed I haven't found out. If she's no longer allowed to carry on her folksy switchboard detective work, I'm certain she's unhappy now and the town has lost some of its spark.

Just as life in the little city of Huntsville is less zestful now that Shorty Hale is gone.

Shorty was a chesty little fellow who stood about five feet four in his high-heeled boots. He ran a secondhand store and a horse and mule lot at Huntsville and he was always threatening to shoot people. I've sat in his store and watched one of Shorty's friends come in and ask him what he was doing and Shorty would pull up real rough-like and say, "Why, don't ask me what I'm doin', man. I'll pull out my pistol and blow your head off."

Well, of course Shorty wasn't about to blow anybody's head off, and everybody knew it. He just liked talking that way, enjoyed acting the part of a tough lawman, which for a long time he was. A city marshal at Gilmer.

And for sixty years he was in the horse and mule business and loved to trade and buy and sell and swap. That is, if a customer had anything to deal with. I remember the time a fellow came in his store and asked to see a pair of second-hand shoes.

"How much money you got?" Shorty asked.

"Ninety cents," the customer said.

"Why, man, that ain't even enough to buy a pair of socks." And Shorty then all but shoved the customer out the door. He didn't believe in standing on ceremony with people who wanted shoes for ninety cents.

Around Huntsville they tell the story of the farmer that bought a blind mule off Shorty. Couple days later he returned with the animal. "Shorty," he said, "I can't use this mule. He falls over the feed trough and runs into fences. Something's wrong with him."

"Naw," Shorty said, "ain't nothin' really wrong with that mule. He just don't care where he's goin'."

But Shorty's gone now. So is Fred Fehrenkamp, who always struck me as a sad man.

For five years I had a habit of slowing down and honking when I passed the old Fehrenkamp home in the little north Colorado County town of Frelsburg. Once in a great while Fred Fehrenkamp would return the greeting with a hesitant wave. He might be moving about in that slow way of his among the outbuildings behind the big house, or standing in the side yard looking up at the cracks in the brick walls of his home.

Sometimes on hot afternoons I'd see him in the open door of the old stone building attached to one side of the house. Just sitting there, looking out over the sloping meadows across the road.

One afternoon when the temperature had climbed up around a hundred degrees, I passed that way and noticed the door to the old building was closed. That didn't seem right because Fehrenkamp slept in that building in summer and always left the door open, not just for ventilation, but also because the house wrens liked to come in and hop around on his bed and build their nests in the old jars and bottles he had.

For maybe a mile or so down the road I thought about the door being closed, and wondered maybe if Fehrenkamp had finally bought him an air-conditioner and was spending the summer in the house.

The next time I went through Frelsburg the door was closed again, so I stopped. The house was closed up. I went to the store at the crossroads and inquired and was told Fred Fehrenkamp had died.

When a friend dies and you hear about it right away, that's of course a sad thing. But it saddens me more when he dies and I don't know about it for months.

Well, maybe it's presumptuous of me to say Fehrenkamp was a friend. I just visited with him two or three times there in the old house. I had him figured as a kind and gentle fellow, intelligent, and talented in ways that people didn't consider very practical. Some of his habits seemed strange. The ways of men who live alone in big old houses often seem strange to those of us who live in noisy groups.

The stone building by the house was once the office of Dr. B. J. Fehrenkamp, Fred's father, who died in 1928. Fred slept there in that office among all the dust-covered bottles and records and books that belonged to the doctor. I remember there was a plaster model of a human skull that rested by Fred's bed. And there were big jars sitting around full of human teeth. Dr. Fehrenkamp was an M.D., but when he began practicing at Frelsburg there wasn't any

[198]

dentist in the area, so he pulled a lot of teeth and, for some reason, saved them all. The shelved walls of the building were lined with containers that the doctor kept his medicines in. Fred made no attempt to keep the place dusted. It seemed everything was just as his father left it.

Fred was always studying. Alone in his big old-fashioned kitchen he'd pore over books on biology, chemistry, astronomy, music. I once wrote down the name of a book he was studying in. It was Hopkins' "Scientific American Cyclopaedia of Formulas." Fred did a lot of art work, too. Not paintings but chiefly pen and ink floral designs, marvelously complex. Must have taken him months to complete one.

One day I remarked to him that he seemed to know a lot about a great many different things (an obvious and somewhat dull remark; Fehrenkamp wasn't easy to talk to), and he smiled a little sadly and said, "Yes, but I'm not the master of any of them. That's just the trouble."

He loved nature's things, such as the house wrens that weren't afraid of him, and the assortment of wildlife that roamed freely about his premises. One morning he was in his kitchen cooking breakfast and happened to notice a huge black tarantula on the window sill. Instead of grabbing a broom and whacking the thing, as you or I would, Fred caught it up gently in a two-pound glass coffee jar. I was in his house a few days after that and there was the tarantula in the jar, sitting in the middle of the dining table where Fred was working. "I enjoy observing it," he explained. At that time he was busy translating into English the huge diploma, almost a yard wide and written in Latin, that his father earned from Jefferson Medical College in Philadelphia in 1876.

I always had the idea that Fred would have preferred living in his father's generation rather than in his own time. He didn't tell me that, though. For all I know he might have been happier and more at peace with himself than most of us. Always said he never got lonely there in the old house, not so long as he had his books to read and his studies to do.

He took me through the house one day. It's a big two-story affair, boxlike construction with columns rising up in front and a porch for both upper and lower floors. The outside walls are of soft old brick, and the mortar has cracked alarmingly in places. The saddest thing I ever heard Fred Fehrenkamp say he said one day when we were standing out in the yard inspecting the mortar cracks. "The old place is falling down," he said, "and I don't know what to do about it."

After I learned of his death I went back to the old house for a while. To me it was a lonely place when Fehrenkamp lived there, and now it's vastly more so. The mass of bushes and trees and vines appears to be supporting the old home, holding it up by thrusting a stem into a crack or curling a tendril about a leaning member of the porch rail. The place belongs now to the mockingbirds that call from high up on the roof gables, and to the wasps and bees and the other flying, crawling things that inhabit its tangled shrubs. I won't stop there again.

But there are other places that still make good stops. I can always go to Trinity and find Runt Carroll sitting in his office there on the main drag, and get him talking about his baseball-playing days. Carroll is a small muscular man about five feet six and a hundred fifty-five pounds. When he talks baseball the fire in his brown eyes gets to smoldering and popping and sizzling, the way it did when he was pitching amateur and semi-pro and finally professional baseball. There are those who'll say the only reason Runt didn't make it to the major leagues is that he insisted on playing every day, and pitchers just don't pitch every day.

But they did when they were on the teams Runt played with.

"I pitched a many a double-header in my time, and eight no-hit games. I was lightning fast."

When Carroll says things like that, they don't sound like boasting but like statements of fact, and before he gets through with you, you'll be convinced the worst thing that ever happened to baseball is that Runt didn't play in the big time.

A few miles up in the Piney Woods from his office, at Weldon, where he grew up, Runt used to lie in bed at night when he was a kid and dream he was Ty Cobb. He learned to hit a curve by swinging a hoe handle at the corncobs chunked at him by other boys who dreamed the same dreams, and he played his first game for money at the age of fourteen. That was when they hung the nickname on him (Ira is his real name), and he remained Runt all his life "because I couldn't quite whip everybody that called me that. But I tried."

Runt worked up to play about a month with Beaumont in the Texas League, and of course he was blowing them down when somebody discovered he was still under contract to some Class C club somewhere, and that's when he quit going up. But he pitched for more than thirty years.

"I didn't start cheatin' until 1926," Runt will tell you. "Before that I didn't have to. But I developed a spitter that would break down like it was falling off a table. The bean ball, now, well, of course I threw at batters, but I always threw at the top of their head. That way they'd go to the dirt and wouldn't get hit. And I'm proud to say that in all my career, and all the guys I threw at, I never once hit one in the head."

One of the memories I'll enjoy in my old age will be the picture of Runt Carroll sitting in a café at Trinity and demonstrating, as he might demonstrate the tying of an intricate knot to a Boy Scout, how to drive phonograph needles into a baseball to weight it on one side and make it do crazy things when it passes over the plate.

Then you ought to stop and meet Edgar Rummel, too.

Rummel is postmaster of a little town called Ledbetter, which most motorists driving between Houston and Austin probably don't even notice as they whiz through. The post office stands a little distance off the highway in a former church house built in 1888. Rummel is somewhere around sixty years old, a bachelor and a remarkably sociable fellow considering he is stone deaf and has been from birth.

Only those in his position know the difficulty a man has in learning to speak when he's never heard a sound. Rummel did it, though, which is characteristic of him. He does everything anybody else does except hear. He clings to an axiom that a man can overcome almost any handicap as long as he refuses to withdraw and become antisocial.

Edgar seems to laugh at the challenge of living in a silent world. He can converse with you first rate if you face up to him so he can read your lips. I expect that learning to read-lip Texans is pretty tough, since so many of us insist on letting about half our sounds come out the nose while holding a stiff upper lip. But Edgar is accustomed to overcoming difficulty and responds to it with astonishing invention.

The alarm clock, for example.

He was having trouble waking up chilly mornings in time to open the post office, so he built a deaf man's alarm. He took the coil out of an old car, hooked it up to a conventional alarm clock, strung tiny wires back and forth across his mattress. When the clock alarmed at the set time, the coil sent a not so mild electric shock through his mattress.

He maintains no man alive will lie abed while that alarm goes off.

People who are supposed to know about such things say Rummel has educated himself at least to the level of a college bachelor's degree. There in the comfortable untidiness of his bachelor's diggings he can sound off at length on theology, mechanics, literature, history, agriculture, psychology, and doubtless various others I've not heard him sound off about. He's a great lover of sports, serves as president of an amateur baseball league, and likes to talk about his own football-playing days at the Texas School for the Deaf at Austin, where a lip-reading girl would steal signals out of the opposition's huddle and pass them to her team via sign language.

One of the year-end pleasures I anticipate is receiving Rummel's Christmas letter.

You understand this letter is not written especially to me. It just happens my name is on Edgar's mailing list. Along with five-hundred-odd other people, I get a mimeographed copy. Though the letter is mailed out at Christmas, it is more in the nature of an annual report on Rummel's family and friends—who has died, who was born, who was sick. Also it deals with the problems and pleasures of being postmaster of Ledbetter, Texas; hunting and vacation and postmaster convention trips; gardening, weddings, fishing, barbecue feasts. All this is recorded in Rummel's special brand of floral prose, which often offers some pretty neat phrases. His most recent report runs ten full legal-sized, single-spaced pages, written on a new electric typewriter that Edgar loves because it doesn't have a carriage and so can't knock his glass off the table like the old one was always doing.

A few samples from the letters:

". . . the Lord has been good to us this year, for despite the drought I had a fine spring garden which furnished

ample and varied eating until the end of July. But thereafter our entire area was like unto the plagues of Egypt,
with swarms of fat grasshoppers which destroyed every living thing, even gnawing off the tops of my Arizona okra
which resists drought and bears until frost. Tried planting
turnips in dry dust; they came up but to die in subsequent
drought . . .

"Rains can be extremely spotty in Central Texas; some
ranges get 2 inches at one end of a 500-acre tract and none
on the other . . . Our county seat a mere 16 miles away
recorded 10 inches less than we for the year, like the tale
of a Texas farmer who left his double-barrel shotgun leaning
against a fence. That night a terrific rain storm came up
. . . Remembering the neglected gun the next morning, the
farmer found the right barrel full of water, but the left was
empty . . ."

Rummel is a great traveler. He keeps notes on the prices
of goods and services in the various states where he goes
and includes this data in his Christmas letters. So that's
how I know that cigarettes were selling for $1.64 a carton
in the state of Oregon in 1960 and in 1962 in the Carousel
Room of Chicago's Hotel Morrison, dinner prices were
"starting at $3.50 but unfortunately not stopping there."

"Tyke and I were sick," Rummel once wrote (Tyke is a
big collie dog that lives with him), "and I took myself to
my doctor and Tyke to the La Grange Veterinary Clinic.
Tyke got better right away while I suffered 10 days longer,
so I told my doc that next time he could treat Tyke and
I'd take my chances at the vet's."

A newcomer to Rummel's mailing list may be dismayed
at attempting to figure out who, among those named in the
letter, is kin to whom, and how. After a year or two you
discover that it doesn't really matter if you'll just relax and
enjoy the news. It happens I am acquainted with a few

Edgar mentions by first name. I know who Toodle is, and Leroy and Elmo and Meredith and Charlie and Don. I've never met Milton or Ernest or Bessie or M.J. or Mother Burgdorff or Gertrude or any of dozens of others Edgar names annually. But all the same I am interested in them, just as you would be if you received Edgar's letter. Maybe you would even rejoice along with all the other recipients to hear that Hub and Gladys found a new home in Fort Worth for six thousand dollars that's better than anything else they looked at for eleven thousand.

Rummel sometimes uses his letter to sound off about things he doesn't like, and tops on this list is a small wedding.

"There were four big country weddings this year but the convention and my hospital stay gave me two misses, to my deep regret, as nothing can match these events for sheer social conviviality, gastronomy and refreshment, all on the basic principle that only too much is ever enough. Not all are like that; some just take the nearest justice and minimum witnesses; others a big church wedding but with the reception known as a 'cake and punch' affair; and lowest on the scale of my personal experience was where the couple made a hurried departure while the sky pilot had the rest of us pinned down with a long and pious prayer, leaving relatives on both sides to get acquainted with each other. They did not!"

About a wedding he attended at nearby Waldeck, Rummel wrote, ". . . I oft danced with the bride's mother and her sisters, all brunettes and all lovely, in the good old days when Waldeck had a dance hall and the adjacent home of the owner featured midnight two-bit suppers, family style, which seemed to refresh the musicians so they could play until near dawn, and when a white handker-

[205]

chief was hung from the center oil lamp after midnight, indicating the subsequent dances were ladies' choice."

Edgar describes life and times at Ledbetter with unflinching candor. One of his Christmas reports included a detailed account of what he entitled "Operation Hernia," meaning his surgical experience in a hospital at Giddings. The account covered all, from a description of just what a hernia is to how it feels to get a hospital enema, as well as how he brought his own brand of medicine to speed recuperation. "I had my hospitality bag filled with Walker's Deluxe, and with many sympathetic and thirsty friends coming in, I used over three fifths during my stay. I did not care for any the first two days, but after that the medical staff was positively astonished by my cheerfulness, morale and quick recovery."

Edgar's card of thanks, sent out to friends after his return home, read in part, "I sincerely and gratefully thank my many friends and relatives for their cards, letters, books, flowers, cheering visits and other acts of helpfulness during my recent stay in the hospital; thanks also to Doc Charlie Burns and the highly attentive nursing staff . . . and to Hiram Walker and Sons for their splendid uplift to my morale . . ."

So you see that knocking around the Gulf Southwest can be rewarding if you know where to stop.

Texas as a whole is a land of extremes—in climate, geology, topography . . . yes, and when it comes to people, too. I could show you notes I took when one day I met, just by chance, and talked with a doctor of philosophy on the street of an East Texas town and then half an hour later met and talked with a completely illiterate person. These two men walk the same streets daily, buy groceries and shirts at the same stores, go to the same theater. Yet their worlds are pole to pole apart.

Now anybody can find a Ph.D. to talk to; it's not as easy to locate an illiterate who'll sit down and discuss his illiteracy. Not that there aren't a good many Texans who can't read and write. There are. But getting them to admit it is something else.

Jimmy Jefferson admitted it. Now that's a fictitious name— the only one in this book. I use it not because Jimmy was hesitant to give his name. He gave it freely. But he has his pride the same as the Ph.D. and you've got to respect that. It doesn't matter where he lives. I found him in the Piney Woods, where he scratches out a living working in the timber. There are thousands more like him, who make the big X when they have to sign their names.

Jimmy's handicap is far worse than Edgar Rummel's. If you held up a big sign to Jimmy that read, "Run for your life," Jimmy wouldn't know what it said.

He's a Negro, twenty-six years old. He has an alert mind, plenty of common sense, an intelligent face, good manners, and a fine muscular physique. But he can't write his name because nobody ever taught him.

I borrowed the office of a friend in the town where Jimmy lives, and we talked a long while about the problems of being illiterate. I asked him if he could recite the alphabet, which was a stupid question because Jimmy doesn't know what the word alphabet means. So I asked if he could say his ABC's. Then he knew.

"No, not too good. I don't think I could do that. The way it was, when I was a little kid I worked. In the field, to help my daddy make a livin'. I had . . . let's see . . . four brothers and . . . six sisters, I think it was. My sister tried to teach me to read when I was little but it didn't help. When I went to school, to the first grade, I was thirteen years old and to tell the truth I was kind of ashamed being so big and all the rest of 'em so little. So I left.

"No, I don't live at home. Sometimes I go to my mother's and eat supper. I guess you could say I don't live anywhere. I just sleep around, first one place and another. Sometimes I sleep in a truck."

Jimmy was working in the timber at the time, hauling pulpwood to the railroad. He was driving a truck illegally, since his illiteracy prevents him from getting a driver's license.

"I'm a pretty good driver. When I see a stop sign I know what it is. I know some of the signs, and I can watch out for myself and for other folks. I don't want to hurt nobody."

When he receives mail Jimmy takes it to his sister and she reads it to him. "You might say then it's not a secret in a way, but in another way it is a secret because nobody knows what the letter says but me and my sister.

"Now I can count pretty good. I can count . . . oh, up to a thousand, maybe two thousand if I kept goin'. And I can count money enough to know prices of things and pay people what I owe."

Jimmy has never filed an income tax return. Said he'd never made enough money. The summer day I saw him he'd worked eight hours loading pulpwood, out in a humid pine bottom where the heat can be something unbearable. He said he'd eaten "a piece of pressed ham and a nickel cooky for dinner." Said he never eats any breakfast, and that he had no money to buy supper that night.

"Lots of times I work all day in the woods without any dinner, without anything to eat all day. Well, sure, I do get weak sometimes. But when I have the money I eat at a café, or buy cold cuts."

I wonder what the nutritionists would have to say about

[208]

a man who loads logs, sometimes for several days running, without anything to eat but a piece of pressed ham and a nickel cooky for lunch. Jimmy said he'd never been sick. Went to a doctor only once in his twenty-six years, when a bumblebee stung him in the eye.

Jimmy said if anybody would offer to teach him he'd like to try to learn to read. But nobody has ever offered.

"If I had me an education maybe I could drive one of them big trucks on the highway and stop at all those places, and then I wouldn't be out in those woods with the ticks and the redbugs and that heavy strain on my back. But I guess it's too late now."

It's difficult for literate people to comprehend what darkness an illiterate lives in. For example there in the office where we talked I picked up a little pamphlet from a rack. It had a simple three-word headline on the outside, in big red letters. I held it up to Jimmy and asked if those words meant anything to him, anything at all.

"No," he said. "It don't mean nothin' to me."

The pamphlet happened to deal with the value of education and the three-word headline that didn't mean anything to Jimmy said, "Stay In School."

I wish you could have been there, to see the pained expression on Jimmy's intelligent features when he studied those red letters and wished they would speak to him as they do to others.

You should have been along, too, the times I rode with John Estes, professional wolf hunter. I've lost track of him now, for he moves about a lot, living where the wolves are making trouble and where ranchers and farmers call for his services. Wolves still abound in many parts of Texas and sometimes they kill calves and lambs and pigs and chickens. And wolves, Estes claimed, will even raid a watermelon patch and tear up every melon in it. And there was the afternoon Estes caught a skunk in one of his wolf traps and he said, "I've heard if you shoot a skunk just the right way, through the lungs, then he can't stink. We'll try it." So he got up close and shot the skunk through the lungs, but it stank anyway. How it did stink.

Then I'd like to have taken you up in the hills of Comal County to see Emma Rieber, who lives alone and shoots deer almost from her front stoop and writes poems on her window shades with the dauber out of a black-shoe-polish bottle. She used to be troubled with housebreakers during her brief absences from home, so she built a trap for them. Filled a sack with heavy rocks and strung it up over the front door in such a way that when the door opened the rocks came down on top of the intruders. And she had the pleasure of hiding in the bushes one night and seeing the trap work beautifully, and after that she wasn't bothered by housebreakers.

And you should have met Madame Rebecca, whom I found doing business at Bellville. She's a Cherokee Indian palmist. People come to her with their "troubles, worries, and doubts" and she gives advice in all affairs. Indian palmists are pretty common in Texas. Madame Rebecca is, so she explained to me, a sort of queen bee among a large group of Cherokees who live in South and East Texas. These Indians hold down jobs and operate businesses like any other citizens, and occasionally they get together for a tribe meeting when Madame gives palm readings to all the members, free of charge.

And C. B. Jamison. He's another you'd have enjoyed. He's a mechanic at Marlin and he wears a little flower in his mouth all the time, from dawn till he goes to bed, except when he eats. Now why would a man do that?

"Well," he said, "I was raised on a farm at Glen Rose, and when I was a boy they'd send me after the horses.

There was a lot of wild flowers along the way and I'd pick 'em, and when I caught the horses I'd need both hands to hold 'em so I'd throw the flowers away. Well, all but one of 'em and I'd put that in my mouth. Pretty soon it got to be a habit. I'm over seventy now and I started it when I was seven. I've been wearin' the flower ever since, and I miss it when it's not there."

Also I wish you could have eaten some of the world's best barbecue with me at Crockett, cooked by a Negro named Arthur Hatch, who kept the hickory fire going in his barbecue pit for thirty solid years day and night, and it didn't die until Arthur did.

And there was Will Weeren, of the little town of Burton, who stood one day out on the boardwalk fronting Burton business houses and recited all four stanzas of the poem *Invictus*. Why? Well, just to show he could do it, and in a loud voice, too, with passers-by watching and listening.

There are a few towns you ought to see, too, just because they've got personality. Towns like Fayetteville, a little village with a Czech background where Chilli Kubena serves lunches to the customers in his café and then at one o'clock rushes across the town square to take up his position as a teller in the bank. And where you can go in Polansky's Confectionery and see ice-cream sodas and bock beer served on the same counter and listen to the customers speak a delightful combination of English and Czech.

And Coldspring, the seat of San Jacinto County, where they have a handsome fence around the courthouse to keep the free-roaming livestock from grazing the shrubbery. I attended the first San Jacinto County Fair held after World War II, and the steers and milk cows on exhibit were tethered on the town square to be judged and the turkeys and chickens were down in the basement of the courthouse. And when I told that in Houston nobody would believe it. But Coldspring is getting citified now, and even has the streets around the courthouse paved.

And then there's Goliad, an old town with huge spreading live oaks standing even out in the streets. They tell about the fellow who rolled into town about three sheets to the wind, plowed into a sturdy live oak growing in the middle of the pavement, was arrested on a D.W.I. charge. "Didn't you see that tree there in the street?" the judge asked him. And the fellow said, "I saw it, Judge, but I just didn't believe it." Just outside Goliad, on the San Antonio River, stands ancient Presidio La Bahia, stone fort built by the Spanish in the eighteenth century and now used as a Catholic church. I stood in the shadow of the presidio and heard A. V. Shaw talk about the $3,500,000 worth of gold and silver he thinks lies hidden near the old fort.

"It's there, all right," Shaw said with that distant look all treasure hunters have. "I know it's there. I've spent half a lifetime and a fortune trying to get it. I've worked on this thing for nearly thirty years."

Work he did, and hard. He traveled, studied, checked out the legend of the fortune in gold and silver, mined in New Mexico by Spaniards and said to be buried at the presidio when Texas was under Spanish rule. He bought land in the area, excavated, slaved, went broke, borrowed, went broke again, still worked. The last report I had, he was still at it.

Or if treasure hunters don't appeal to you, I can show you a washer-pitching game that's been in progress on the yard of the Shelby County Courthouse for half a century, and a running domino game at Woodville that's almost as old if not older.

Or we could go to Ellinger and get Walter Koehl to tell us how to make a pie out of blackbirds. Most early springs, blackbirds in fluttering armies numbering tens of thousands spread over the landscape.

"Best place to get blackbirds is around a feed lot, where you have thousands of 'em in a bunch. What we do, we get three men with shotguns and Number Nine shot. When they're thick enough, one man can knock down a dishpan full of birds in one shot.

"Course there's not much to a blackbird but the breast. We just yank that out and throw the rest away. Leaves you a piece of meat about the size of a half dollar. We boil 'em first and then bake 'em into a pie, just like any meat pie."

You don't care for blackbird pie?

Well, then, we can always go out on Oxford Street in Houston and listen to Joe Jenkins talk about his days as a wrangler in West Texas, when it seemed he was always running to keep from plowing behind a mule. How he hated that plowing. It ran him out of East Texas when he was a boy.

"One spring my pa sent me out to round up the horses to plow and told me not to come back without 'em. Well, I couldn't find them danged horses because they'd gone home while I was lookin' for 'em. So I just kept aheadin' into the sun, a way out west where the Mexicans did all the grubbin' and there weren't no stumps and trees to hoe around. About a year from then I wrote home and told Pa I hadn't found them horses yet but soon's I ever did I'd drive 'em in, and I didn't go home till I'd grown up and too big for Pa to jump me. That's my story, and I stick with it."

People like Joe Jenkins (who can use better English than that when he cares to) and J. Henry Martindale and Pat Craddock and Drayton Speights and J. B. Choate and

Mangy Springer and all the others perform what to me is a great service to the people of my state—that is, they help preserve some of the fun of being a Texan.

Because being a Texan is not nearly so much fun as it was even fifteen years ago. Texans as a whole once enjoyed insulting their own state, and acting generally like the country folks most of them still are. We used to call it bragging. It wasn't really bragging.

We got a kick out of repeating the old phrase credited to General Sheridan, in which he said if he owned hell and Texas he'd rent out Texas and live in hell. We enjoyed talking about how terrible our weather is. We told the joke about the Eastern traveler who asked the old rancher, "Does the wind blow this way all the time?" And the rancher answered, "No, sometimes it blows the other way." We said our sandstorms, our northers, our tornadoes, our floods, and our droughts were the world's worst. We said our men were the ugliest and our steaks the toughest. And we poked fun at the Texas brand of justice, and, to illustrate, we told the yarn about the blacksmith who shot a man, but since he was the only blacksmith in town the local citizens hanged a shoemaker for the crime because they had two shoemakers and could get along with just one. I think people of other states didn't really resent this kind of bragging as long as it was done in the right way.

Now it's true a lot of Texans never learned to do it right. We've still got some of those. They are the loudmouths that haven't helped our image—the ones who think that when they leave the boundaries of the state they've got to "act like a Texan" and talk loud and tell lies about how big everything is at home. (Alaska, thank the powers, has helped that situation a lot.) Still I fear we yet produce a sizable annual crop of professional Texans with money who go to New York or Los Angeles and wear fancy boots and big hats and buy drinks for the house and talk about "my lil ol' ranch back in Texiz."

Since these are the ones making all the noise, it's tough to convince the world that they are in the minority. The true and the faithful citizen of my state abhors the professional Texan because he is the worst of all things—a phony—and doesn't have sense enough to know it.

But the old self-deprecating Texas brag was a good thing, because it was Texas humor and not really boasting. I grieve that this attitude is fading.

Why is it fading? Because of the almighty dollar, that's why.

Gradually, following World War II, the Texas business community quit laughing about the old-style Texas boasts and began crying about them. Merchants saw that receipts would be better if Texas had something besides cotton, cows, oil, sheep, goats, hound dogs, tenant farmers, and a reputation for bragging. So they reorganized their chambers of commerce and printed up brochures extolling the merits of their towns and sent them up East for the industrialists to read. There's no trace of old-style Texas humor in a chamber-of-commerce brochure now. It speaks of the sunny climate (not the hot weather) and the mild winters (not the sudden northers and the hard freezes) and the natural resources (not the ugly men). I have to grin at the brochure that quotes a Texas community's "average temperature" at seventy-two degrees. It reminds me of the old story about the fellow who somehow managed to drown in a creek the average depth of which was one foot, the stream being ten feet deep in the middle but shallow as a bird bath at the edge. I know some spots in Texas where the average temperature is seventy-two degrees, all right, but ranges from a hundred fourteen degrees in August to three below zero in January.

But we mustn't mention such matters any longer, because don't you see if we speak of how bad the hurricane was it might scare off an industry with a big payroll. And we mustn't make jokes about Texas justice because that would sound bad to New York investment bankers. So instead we speak of how we have symphonies and operas and art museums and beautiful churches.

I liked the other way better.